Twenty + One

21 Short Stories

SERIES III

A Tapestry of Truths, Trials, and Tender Triumphs

SHREE SHAMBAV

Twenty + One

21 Short Stories SERIES III

Shree Shambav

Published by Shree Shambav, Tamil Nadu, India

First Edition, 2025

ISBN: 978-93-343-5125-5

Email:shreeshambav@gmail.com

Web:www.shambav.org

DEDICATION

"Isavasyam idam sarvam yat kim ca jagatyam jagat, tena tyaktena bhunjitha, ma gridhah kasyasvid dhanam"

To the Almighty,

the Divine Masters,

the family who listens,

and my parents who see –

your presence shapes the pages of my life's journey.

"Isavasyam idam sarvam yat kim ca jagatyam jagat"

Meaning: "God encompasses everything you perceive, see, or touch with your sense organs."

DISCLAIMER

The *Twenty + One* book series unfolds as a heartfelt exploration of existence, a tapestry woven with reflections on the Creator and the Creatrix—Mother Nature. Rooted in lived experiences and distilled wisdom, this work seeks not to dictate truth but to offer perspectives that may resonate, challenge, or inspire. Each realisation embraced by the reader becomes a cherished moment of insight, a seed of wisdom blooming along their own journey.

Crafted with sincerity, this book stands as an offering of love, compassion, kindness, and care—the very forces that shape and sustain life. It does not impose a singular understanding but instead invites contemplation, allowing each soul to interpret its words through the lens of personal experience.

Each story within the *Twenty + One* series serves as a testament to the beauty of life, a call to honour the delicate balance of nature, and a reminder that all beings share the right to exist in harmony within this vast and interconnected world. Through story-based wisdom, this work echoes the teachings of revered Masters who have safeguarded truth across time, traditions, and cultures.

At its core, this book seeks to impart a message of deep empathy, unity, and awareness, fostering a connection to the self, to humanity, and the natural world. No part of its content or arrangement is intended to provoke harm, discomfort, or discord. Should any element unintentionally unsettle, it remains purely incidental and never by design.

Readers are encouraged to approach these pages with openness, understanding that the insights shared arise from a singular perspective, offered not as absolutes but as gentle invitations to reflection. These words are not directives, but guiding lights—meant to spark thought, stir the heart, and accompany each seeker on their own unfolding path.

May these stories serve as a source of warmth, wisdom, and wonder, illuminating new depths of understanding and enriching the journey of those who seek meaning within them.

Note - If any part of the book, in any sequence, hurts the reader's sentiments, it would be just out of a sheer accident, not intentional

Tapestry of Silent Triumphs

"In the quiet corners of everyday life lie stories often left untold—fragments of courage, tenderness, and unspoken dreams. *Twenty + One – 21 Short Stories Series III* is not merely a collection of fiction; it is a sacred vessel of lived truths, distilled from the invisible struggles and subtle victories that define the human journey.

Each tale is a thread in a greater tapestry, woven with the emotions we dare not name—grief that lingers in empty rooms, love that hides behind silence, hope that rises like dawn after a sleepless night. These stories do not shout; they whisper. And in that whisper, the soul listens, remembers, and heals.

Within these pages, you won't find heroes wearing crowns—you'll find them in mothers who wait without complaint, in strangers who give without asking, in children who dream despite the world's weight. Shree Shambav invites us to witness the sacred in the ordinary, the divine in the broken, and the light that dances even in the shadow's depth.

This book is a mirror, not of who we appear to be—but of who we truly are when the world quiets and the heart speaks. It is for those who have lost and still choose to love, who have fallen yet continue to rise, and for every soul that has ever yearned to be seen and understood.

Let these stories hold you. Let them open you. For in their simplicity lies a profound truth: life's smallest moments often leave the deepest mark."

– Shree Shambav

EPIGRAM

"In the tempest of life's storms, hidden within the thunderous clouds, lie transformative opportunities. These tumultuous moments, though daunting, are portals to resilience, strengths unbeknownst, and the shimmering silver linings of growth. Instead of succumbing to the ferocity of challenges, let us embrace the alternate facets of life's storms, emerging not broken but fortified. Navigating the turbulent seas of existence demands courage, hope, and an unwavering belief in the beauty that awaits beyond the storm clouds. Life's storms are not the conclusion; they are chapters sculpting us into resilient, potent, and compassionate beings. Therefore, let us confront the storms with confidence, knowing that on the other side, myriad possibilities and hidden dimensions eagerly await our discovery."

– Shree Shambav

Twenty + One

21 Short Stories

SERIES III

Shree Shambav

Shree Shambav is a 50x best-selling author renowned for his transformative works in personal development and spiritual growth.

Dear Cherished Readers

Dear Cherished Readers,

As I embark on this new literary voyage, my heart swells with profound gratitude and an overwhelming sense of connection. With deep emotion, I extend my heartfelt appreciation to each of you who has joined me on this journey.

With sincere warmth, I invite you to revisit the steps we have taken together through the pages of my earlier works. Our odyssey began with "Journey of Soul - Karma," a book that marked my first foray into the world of words and a testament to the raw passion that ignited my writing adventure.

The subsequent chapters of our shared journey unfolded through the enchanting tapestry of the *"Twenty + One"* series. With each page turned, it felt as though a brushstroke was added to the canvas of our collective imagination—stories and sentiments woven to echo within the quiet corners of your heart. These weren't just words; they were invitations to feel, to reflect, and to remember what truly matters.

And how can I not cherish the transformative path we walked together through the *'Life Changing Journey—Inspirational Quotes Series?"* Day by day, quote by quote, we ventured inward—into spaces often overlooked—to find wisdom in simplicity and light in life's shadows. Each reflection was offered as a gentle whisper of hope, a spark meant to uplift, inspire, and remind us that even in silence, the soul speaks.

The release of "Death - Light of Life and the Shadow of Death" promises to shed new light on the timeless mystery of death.

The **Optimum Python Series** is a comprehensive guide designed to empower readers at every stage of their programming journey. It begins with *Series I: Ultimate Guide for Beginners*, which lays a strong foundation in Python, making it accessible and engaging for newcomers. *Series II: Exploring Data Structures and Algorithms* takes the next step, offering a deep dive into core computer science principles that enhance problem-solving skills and coding efficiency. Building on this, *Series III: Python Power for Data Science* introduces powerful libraries such as NumPy, Pandas, Matplotlib, and Scikit-learn, guiding readers through data manipulation, visualisation, and foundational machine learning techniques. Finally, *Series IV: Unleashing the Potential of Data Science with Machine Learning Techniques* explores advanced machine learning models and real-world applications, enabling readers to harness the full potential of data-driven insights. Whether you're just starting out or looking to master sophisticated tools and strategies, this series is your roadmap to Python proficiency and beyond.

Shree Shambav expands his artistic repertoire with "*Whispers of Eternity: A Symphony of Soulful Verses*," a heartfelt exploration of the human experience. Alongside this, his "*Whispers of the Soul: A Journey Through Haiku*" distils profound insights into poignant verses. Together, these works showcase his versatility and mastery of soulful expression, inviting readers on a journey of self-discovery. Through his poetry, he weaves a rich tapestry of emotion that resonates deeply with the heart.

Shree Shambav's latest works—*Learn to Love Yourself: A Journey of Discovering Inner Beauty and Strength Through 10 Transformative Rules, The Power of Letting Go: Embrace Freedom and Happiness, A Journey of Lasting Peace—are true treasures of self-discovery, The Entitlement Trap: Get Over It, Get On, Whispers of a Dying Soul: Unspoken Regrets and Unlived Dreams, Whispers of Silence - Unlocking Inner Power through Stillness, The Power of Words: Transforming Speech, Transforming Lives, The Art of Intentional Living: Minimalism for a Life of Purpose, Awakening the Infinite:The Power of Consciousness in Transforming Life, Beyond the Veil: A Journey Through Life After Death series, Bonds Beyond Blood - Where love builds bridges, and bonds defy blood., A Journey into Spiritual Maturity - 12 Golden Rules for Inner*

Transformation, The Seeker's Gold : Unlocking Life's Greatest Treasure, , The Power of Manifestation - Unlocking The Path From Thought To Reality, Born to Rise Series and The Law of Attraction.

In addition to these works, Shree Shambav has recently ventured into astrology with the release of Astrology Unveiled – Foundations of Ancient Wisdom Series I to VIII, expanding into the realm of metaphysics. These books explore the foundational principles of Vedic astrology, offering readers a rich and practical understanding of this ancient wisdom.

Your unwavering support, enthusiasm to immerse yourself in my writings, and readiness to embark on these journeys with me have been my greatest sources of inspiration. Your input has been a beacon guiding me through the creation process, moulding these stories into containers of passion, emotion, knowledge, and resonance.

As I unveil this new narrative before you, know that your presence, insights, and shared moments have been my companions. The path we have walked together is etched in the annals of my creative evolution, and it's an honour beyond words to have you by my side once more.

Here's to the readers who have illuminated my path with their presence, who have embraced my stories with open hearts, and who have woven themselves into the very fabric of my literary world. Our journey has been a symbiotic dance of writer and reader, a harmony of souls brought together by the magic of storytelling.

With a heart brimming with appreciation and eyes glistening with anticipation, I extend my deepest gratitude for your unwavering support. Thank you for the memories, the shared emotions, and the countless hours spent in the worlds we've crafted together. As we step into this new adventure, let's continue to explore, feel, and discover the boundless horizons that words can unveil.

Warmly,

Shree Shambav

Suggested Reads

FROM BEST-SELLING AUTHOR

Endorsements

The first story itself will make you want to read more. How true that "A beggar will always be a beggar, even if you give him the entire world," Shambav narrates a thoughtful tale.

We, humans, are judgmental always. Why do we not accept people the way they are? If a person is greedy, even abundance is never sufficient for him. The author, through meaningful stories, has tried his best to convey various life lessons. Nobody is superior here. And nobody has the right to make you feel inferior until you give them that opportunity.

The Taj Mahal wasn't constructed in a day; good things will take a lot of time. It all starts with small steps. We become what we think. So one needs to have a positive apppositiveoward life.

Every story has got a title and a quote which brings more curiosity to begin reading the story. And the illustrations are also meaningful and alluring.

Throughout the book, one thing is highlighted, i.e whatever we do will return in one way or the other way. Nobody is superior here. We are all interrelated and interlinked. One needs to remember to be happy with whatever we have.

And loving ourselves first is the greatest wisdom that one can have.

Overall, a beautiful collection.

Nandini (Educationalist)

About the Author

Shree Shambav is an internationally acclaimed best-selling author, inspirational speaker, artist, philanthropist, life coach, strategist and entrepreneur. A world record holder, his deep passion for music led him to create soul-stirring albums, drawing inspiration from his celebrated poetry collection, Whispers of Eternity. His profound insights have sparked deep personal transformations, guiding countless individuals toward self-discovery, purposeful living, and authenticity.

With an extraordinary ability to unlock human potential, Shree empowers individuals to break through limitations and embrace their highest selves. His writings, lectures, and compassionate guidance continue to uplift lives, fostering resilience, mindfulness, and personal growth.

Shree Shambav is a 50x best-selling author celebrated for his profound contributions to personal development and spiritual growth.

Shree Shambav's literary journey took flight with the celebrated Journey of Soul - Karma, where he delved into the depths of human experience to unveil profound insights. Garnering recognition through multiple literature awards, his repertoire includes esteemed works, such as the Twenty + One Series, and the enlightening Life Changing Journey – Inspirational Quotes series.

As a distinguished alumnus of the Indian Institute of Management and the National Institute of Technology, Shree Shambav brings a wealth of corporate acumen from his tenure in multinational corporations. His most recent publications, including Unveiling the Enigma, Death - Light of Life and the Shadow of Death and Optimum – Power Python Series I, Series II, Series III and Series IV, demonstrate his mastery of both the literary and technical spheres.

Shree Shambav expands his artistic repertoire with "*Whispers of Eternity: - A Symphony of Soulful Verses*," a heartfelt exploration of the human experience. Alongside this, his "*Whispers of the Soul: A Journey Through Haiku*" distils profound insights into poignant verses. Together, these works showcase his versatility and mastery of soulful expression, inviting readers on a journey of self-discovery. Through his poetry, he weaves a rich tapestry of emotion that resonates deeply with the heart.

Shree Shambav's latest works—*Learn to Love Yourself: A Journey of Discovering Inner Beauty and Strength Through 10 Transformative Rules, The Power of Letting Go: Embrace Freedom and Happiness, A Journey of Lasting Peace—are true treasures of self-discovery, The Entitlement Trap: Get Over It, Get On, Whispers of a Dying Soul: Unspoken Regrets and Unlived Dreams, Whispers of Silence - Unlocking Inner Power through Stillness, The Power of Words: Transforming Speech, Transforming Lives, The Art of Intentional Living: Minimalism for a Life of Purpose, Awakening the Infinite:The Power of Consciousness in Transforming Life, Beyond the Veil: A Journey Through Life After Death series, Bonds Beyond Blood - Where love builds bridges, and bonds defy blood., A Journey into Spiritual Maturity - 12 Golden Rules for Inner Transformation, The Seeker's Gold : Unlocking Life's Greatest Treasure, The Power of Manifestation - Unlocking The Path From Thought To Reality, Born to Rise Series and The Law of Attraction.*

In addition to these works, Shree Shambav has recently ventured into astrology with the release of Astrology Unveiled – Foundations of Ancient Wisdom Series I to VIII, expanding into the realm of metaphysics. These books explore the foundational principles of Vedic astrology, offering readers a rich and practical understanding of this ancient wisdom.

Shree Shambav established the Ayur Rakshita Foundation, which is dedicated to promoting boundless growth, universal fraternity, and environmental protection. The charity helps diverse communities while working for societal progress.

To learn more about Shree Shambav and his works, visit his website at www.shambav.org. For information about the Ayur Rakshita Foundation and its initiatives, visit www.shambav-ayurrakshita.org.

Let's Follow him on Social Media: **@shreeshambav**

Main: https://linktr.ee/shreeshambav

Website: https://www.shambav.org/

LinkedIn: https://www.linkedin.com/in/shreeshambav/

Blog: https://blog.shambav.org/

Instagram: https://www.instagram.com/shreeshambav/

YouTube: https://www.youtube.com/@shreeshambav

Amazon: https://www.amazon.com/author/shreeshambav

Goodreads: https://www.goodreads.com/author/show/22367436.Shree_Shambav

PREFACE

Embarking on the journey of "Twenty + One - 21 Short Stories Series III" invites you to rediscover the enchanting tapestry of storytelling—a timeless voyage that begins in childhood and resonates across the spectrum of life. This collection is more than a compilation of narratives; it's a celebration of the magical realm where tales shape our thoughts, inspire reflection, and foster a sense of belonging.

In the intricate dance of life, stories serve as a universal silver lining, etching profound imprints on the canvas of our minds. From the cherished tales of folklore, Puranas, Mahabharata, and Ramayana, to the captivating narratives of fairy tales, this series encapsulates the richness of our cultural inheritance. The echoes of bedtime stories, narrated by parents and grandparents, linger as evergreen memories, forming the bedrock of familial bonds.

As we traverse through the terrain of the series, we encounter childhood favourites—Snow White, Cinderella, Tarzan, The Jungle Book, Arabian

Nights—now reincarnated through movies and animations. These timeless tales, like ancient treasures slightly tampered with, continue to captivate hearts, imparting lessons on ethics, emotions, values, and the perennial struggle between good and evil.

Children absorb these narratives, stepping into the shoes of heroes, challengers, saviours, gods, and sages. The stories nurture high self-esteem and confidence, shaping not only their characters but also the essence of their being.

Yet, as the pages turn and we grow older, so do our responsibilities. Detaching from certain situations or emotions becomes a challenge when worry or hurt encircles us. In these moments, a subtle shift in perspective becomes a lifeline. The stories within act as magical wands, offering solutions and ready reckoners. Revisiting these tales provides suggestions and perspectives that define our lives, offering solace and insight.

Much like street plays serve as knowledge banks for the uneducated, these stories simplify the complexities of governance, politics, and societal growth. Their enduring popularity through history, drama, theatre, cinema, animation, and series is a testament to their timeless relevance, now further propelled by technology.

Fables, parables, children's tales, and reading as a habit are not merely avenues of learning; they are timeless and joyous portals that open new perspectives. Within these pages, we invite you to traverse these paths, to rediscover the joy of learning and to embrace the wisdom they offer.

Twenty + One - 21 Short Stories Series III" unveils a collection of 21 powerful and inspirational tales that delve into various facets of life. From the relentless pursuit of earthly ambitions to the nurturing haven of unconditional love, the quest for happiness, the tapestry of sufferings, the enchanting beauty of nature, the celebration of diversity, the enduring resilience of kindness, the exploration of truth, and the triumphant moments in life—each story is a poignant exploration of the human experience. Join us on this literary journey as we navigate through the intricate landscapes of existence, finding inspiration and wisdom in every tale.

"As you immerse yourself in these narratives, feel the gentle embrace of nostalgia, reminding us that we were all once wide-eyed children—cherish the days spent weaving dreams and laughter, forever etched in the tapestry of our hearts."

Let the journey unfold.

With gratitude and encouragement,

Shree Shambav

INTRODUCTION

In a world overtaken by the ephemeral glow of digital screens, Shree Shambav extends a compelling invitation to retreat into the tactile embrace of inked narratives. The timeless wisdom encapsulated in the adage 'To make your message sink in, say it with ink' echoes profoundly in the tangible pages of this hard copy—a testament to the enduring power of the written word. "Twenty + One – 21 Short Stories Series III" stands not just as a collection, but as an exploration of the intricate dance between nature's magnificence and the nuances of human character.

This literary treasure trove, comprised of twenty-one captivating stories, delves deep into the threads of human experience. From the weighty symphony in "Story One: Burden" to the intricate pursuit of desires in "Story Two: Busy Chasing," Shree Shambav guides readers through a rich tapestry of emotions, unravelling life's poignant moments.

Beyond mere narratives, these stories serve as mirrors reflecting the complexities of relationships, the quest for happiness, and the transformative resilience inherent in the human spirit. Tales like "The Nest of

Unconditional Love" and "Life is a Mirror" artfully explore familial bonds, the reflective nature of life, and the pursuit of genuine desires beyond superficial goals.

As the narrative unfolds, themes of friendship, self-realisation, and simplicity emerge. Shree Shambav imparts wisdom through tales like "True Friendship" and "A Beautiful Flower," where simplicity and virtuous thinking pave the way for a fulfilling existence.

In stories like "Harmony Amidst Diversity" and "The Resilience of Kindness," the collection underscores the importance of contentment, kindness, and compassion in the pursuit of genuine happiness. These tales echo the belief that the goodness we spread inevitably returns—a profound measure of success.

The transformative power of faith takes centre stage in "King and A Monk," emphasising that faith goes beyond knowledge, beckoning individuals towards a profound transformation in their approach to existence. Each story contributes to a grand tapestry that celebrates the simplicity of living fully in each moment, as highlighted in "A Journey Through Valleys of Wisdom."

The book culminates in a crescendo of resilience, empathy, and compassion in stories like "Resilience Unveiled," "A Tapestry of Life's Triumphs," and "A

Journey Through Suffering's Tapestry." The concluding poem, "A Symphony of Soulful Suffering," delves into the transformative nature of suffering and the profound lessons it imparts.

"Twenty + One – 21 Short Stories Series III" is more than a mere book; it is a primer for life. It invites those seeking to revive their existence to embrace the "Best Practices of Life," to find joy in giving and caring and discover fulfilment through frugal existence. In an era marked by diseases, food crises, conflicts, and hegemony, Shree Shambav's collection serves as a gentle reminder that nature, enduring and resilient, deserves reciprocal care and reverence from humanity—an invitation to repay Mother Nature for the endurance it has generously bestowed upon us. As readers immerse themselves in this literary odyssey, they embark on a journey of introspection, compassion, and resilience—a journey that may leave an indelible mark on their hearts and minds.

With love and gratitude,

PROLOGUE

The Soul of Twenty + One – 21 Short Stories Series III

At the heart of *Twenty + One – 21 Short Stories Series III* lies a quiet, profound truth: that the human experience, in all its complexity, cannot be explained—it must be felt. Each story is not merely written; it is lived. These pages do not just hold words—they hold wounds, memories, unspoken longings, and the quiet radiance of hope that refuses to die.

This collection is a mirror to the soul. Within it, we encounter the silent strength of those who suffer with grace, the tender ache of love left unspoken, and the fragile resilience that blooms in the darkest corners of loss. Here, a father's quiet sacrifices echo louder than thunder; a child's belief becomes a sacred anthem; an old woman's vigil at a temple step becomes a monument to undying love. These are not just stories—they are souls laid bare.

You will walk through landscapes both intimate and immense: the hush of forgotten villages, the chaos of crowded trains, the stillness of hospital corridors, the silence after goodbye. Some stories will cradle you in nostalgia—soft, familiar, and comforting like the scent of home. Others will unsettle you, opening your eyes to truths you'd rather not see, but must. And some will simply ask you to stop—to breathe, to feel, and to remember what it means to be human.

Each tale is a candle flickering against the dark, illuminating truths too often buried beneath the noise of everyday life. In these moments—these fragile, fleeting windows—we are reminded that we are not alone. That our struggles, though silent, are shared. That the smallest gestures often carry the deepest meaning.

This is a book that does not shout for your attention. It whispers. And in those whispers, you may hear echoes of yourself—your joys, your regrets, your secret hopes. Twenty + One is not just a series of stories. It is a sanctuary. A remembrance. A return.

May these stories not merely pass through your mind—but settle in your heart. May they stir what lies dormant, awaken what was lost, and remind you that even in the brokenness, there is beauty. Even in the silence, there is song.

With hope and love,

Shree Shambav

CONTENTS

Burden

"Expectations are the seeds that nurture the growth of reliance in the garden of life; however, if left unchecked, this reliance may blossom into the heavy flowers of burden and the intricate vines of entanglement."

- *Shree Shambav*

During their long journey, Shree Shambav and his disciples came across an elderly gentleman who was crippled by lameness and disease. He meekly sought help, gripped by thirst and hunger. Compelled by compassion, Shree Shambav and one of his dedicated followers interrupted their journey, bringing nourishment and life-giving water to the sick man.

Amid this poignant encounter, a devotee by the name of Pradeep couldn't help but voice his curiosity. With genuine concern gracing his words, Pradeep gently inquired about the elderly man's solitude, questioning the absence of a support system. The old man's eyes, brimming with emotion, met Pradeep's gaze as he began to share his story.

Tears glistened in the old man's eyes as he began to speak, "I once stood as a prosperous and esteemed merchant within this village. Alongside my beloved wife, we nurtured two children with unwavering care and boundless love. The warmth of our family bond was palpable, and our children's respect was a testament to the nurturing we provided. However, the winds of fate shifted when my wife's life was claimed by illness after their marriage. Her departure cast a shadow of sorrow upon my heart, extinguishing my passion for life. In the beginning, my children attended to me with utmost devotion, especially after I entrusted them with my properties. Yet, over time, a change befell them. Slowly, I transformed from a cherished parent into a burden they could no longer bear."

On a serene day, my children requested I part ways with my possessions, and now I stand alone, devoid of care.

Upon hearing the poignant chronicle woven by the old man's voice, Pradeep extended his compassionate presence, a balm to the wounds etched deep within the elderly heart. With shared understanding, they embarked on their onward journey, leaving behind a tapestry of empathy in their wake.

Continuing their travels, they encountered a young boy adorned in tattered garments, his demeanour that of a beggar seeking sustenance. Their journey paused as they approached the boy, and with hearts filled with compassion, they gave upon him a portion of their nourishment.

Pradeep inquired, "You appear youthful; what has led you to the path of begging?"

The young lad shared, "I entered this world within a respectable family where my parents lavished me with care. Our family radiated happiness not long ago. We once embarked on a journey to a nearby destination—my father, mother, sister, and I. As dusk descended during our return, fate dealt us a cruel blow. A grievous accident shattered our lives. I remained unconscious for three days, only to awaken to a world bereft of kin. My family was no more, and in the initial aftermath, my relatives extended their care. Yet, as time unfurled its wings, their warmth transformed into a sense of burden, leaving me in the destitution I find myself today. It is the hand of destiny that has guided my path."

Having listened to the young boy's narrative, they resumed their expedition. In the distance, a middle-aged man caught their attention, his countenance etched with concern. Pradeep approached him, pausing their journey, and gently inquired, "What weighs heavily on your heart?"

The man responded, "In our youth, my brother and I shared an unbreakable bond. Our days were filled with shared laughter, play, and a camaraderie akin to close friends. As time marched forward, our connection waned, and his demeanour transformed following his marriage. With the passing of our parents, he claimed the properties they had bestowed upon me, leaving me bereft of wealth. The absence of possessions or riches does not sadden me; instead, my heart aches for the loss of my brother's companionship. His affection has withered away, replaced by bitter resentment, and I find myself treated as though I am insignificant."

Pradeep's emotions swirled in a mixture of distress and intrigue, his thoughts a labyrinth of inquiries. He grappled with a cascade of questions, each one a testament to his inner turmoil. He contemplated, "How is it possible for children to cast aside their father, despite inheriting his toil and benefiting from his guidance? Why do kinship ties falter when a young boy seeks support? And what could drive brothers who were once inseparable to drift apart?"

Shree Shambav discerned a sense of discontent in Pradeep's demeanour, sensing that he was perturbed by some unresolved query.

In a gentle tone, Shree Shambav shared his wisdom with Pradeep, remarking, "Pradeep, the path of expectation can sometimes lead to disillusionment, yet paradoxically, the very intention behind facing disappointment might steer you towards your aspirations. When you harbour no expectations, you shield yourself from disappointment's sting. It's wise not to form strong attachments, for attachments tend to nurture expectations, and expectations often breed disappointments. Instead, you can anticipate life's offerings while maintaining a stance of non-attachment. Remember, there are two avenues to happiness: either enhance your reality or temper your expectations. It's crucial to grasp that expectation is the wellspring from which frustration and disappointment flow."

"Allow me to tell you a story," Shree Shambav said. "In a time that has long since slipped into the annals of history, a small family—a mother and her devoted son—resided on the far side of a lush jungle. Each day, their livelihood was woven from the threads of nature itself, as they diligently gathered dry twigs and timber. These humble findings held the promise of sustenance, their destiny intertwined with a distant marketplace on the other side of the verdant expanse. Tasked with this mission, young Jayaram, the son, bore the weight of their hopes and dreams, shouldering the gathered timber as he ventured through the depths of the dense forest. A ritual of resilience unfolded with the passing days—his journey to the marketplace, the exchange of his efforts for essentials, and his return home before the sun dipped below the horizon, guided by the rhythm of the surrounding wilderness."

On a certain day, Jayram found himself disheartened as his attempts to sell his goods before dusk proved futile. As the sun dipped lower on the horizon, casting gradual darkness, a sense of concern loomed—he was confronted with the challenge of transporting his wares back. With bated breath, he waited, his hope flickering in the fading light. Almost at the brink of despair, a figure emerged, hastening toward him with purpose. Gratitude painted the man's words as he expressed, "I had feared a lack of timber for tonight's cooking, yet your dedication to staying late has eased my worry. Thank you."

The man bought the timber and paid him happily. Meanwhile, the place was covered with darkness; the stars were twinkling in the sky. Jayaram was worried about how he would travel alone in the jungle. So Jayaram waited for someone to join him so that he would have a companion to cross the jungle.

The man bought the timber and paid him with a cheerful countenance. In the backdrop, darkness had settled in, and the sky was adorned with glimmering stars. Jayaram found himself engulfed in concern regarding his solitary journey through the jungle. With trepidation gripping his thoughts, he opted to bide his time, yearning for a fellow traveller who could offer companionship and assist him in traversing the challenging expanse of the forest.

After enduring hours of anticipation and subsequent letdown, a profound worry settled within him. He grappled with the uncertainty of what lay ahead if no one were to arrive. Anxiety gnawed at him—how would he find his way back through the enveloping darkness of the jungle? Would he encounter the threat of wild animals or suffer the sting of venomous creatures and insects? The pitch-black surroundings conjured fears of inadvertently stumbling into pits or injuring oneself through falls. His mind swirled with doubts and confusion, a tumultuous storm of thoughts. A deep yearning for assistance consumed him. Amidst the weight of these concerns, a glimmer of hope pierced the darkness—he spotted a distant light, barely discernible, and the faint outline of a man's face. Drawing nearer to the source of illumination, his heart raced with anticipation.

Jayaram inquired, "Could you kindly share your destination?"

The man responded, "I'm on my way back home, although I must traverse this dense and shadowy jungle."

Jayaram's heart brimmed with joy upon hearing this, and he inquired, "Would it be possible for me to accompany you, considering my home lies along the same path?"

A chuckle escaped the man's lips as he replied, "Certainly, I welcome your company."

A wave of relief swept over Jayaram, dissolving his worries and filling him with happiness. He sensed the hours spent waiting had yielded a meaningful reward. Inwardly, he affirmed, "I am secure now, and I hold the certainty of arriving safely at my home."

Following an extended journey, they reached a juncture where the man came to a halt and remarked, "Jayaram, I must veer to the right from this point." With those words, he resumed his travels.

Jayaram continued in the leftward direction, having completed only half of their journey. Faced with this situation, confusion enveloped him; the darkness ahead left him at a loss, unsure of how to proceed.

Jayaram's self-reproach took hold, his inner dialogue echoing, "I ought to have remained at the marketplace; I should have held back my trust in this individual. At the very least, I should have sought a comprehensive account of his route. Carrying a torch would have been a prudent decision. Can I possibly find my way home? Countless 'what ifs'..."

After a prolonged contemplation, Jayaram set forth on his journey. Anxious beads of sweat mingled with shivers, and his heart raced with an intensity that reverberated through his being. Every step seemed to echo his self-reproach. Amid his travels, his forehead collided with an overhanging tree branch, eliciting a sharp cry of pain. A distant animal's call pierced the air, instantly dispelling his discomfort. Instinct propelled him forward, his pace quickening. As the sound drew nearer, he broke into a run, navigating the darkness with urgency. Alas, his frantic sprint led him to an unfortunate tumble into a concealed pit, his legs and hands bearing the brunt of the impact. The once-frenzied sounds receded, leaving behind an eerie silence. Slowly extricating himself from the pit, Jayaram pressed onward with newfound determination, his pace swift and unwavering. Finally, he arrived home, after his arduous journey.

Upon stepping inside his dwelling, Jayaram's gaze fell upon his mother, who patiently awaited his return. Her voice carried concern as she inquired, "What has befallen you that you wear such an air of urgency?"

Jayaram recounted all the unfolding events to his mother, sharing every detail of his journey. In response, his mother gently advised, "First, cleanse yourself," and then offered him nourishment to satiate his hunger.

Following an extended stretch of silence, his mother spoke, "Embrace self-reliance by aligning your actions with your discernment. Your achievements in life are fundamentally shaped by your efforts, surpassing any external influences. You cannot linger, hoping for someone else to come to your aid; on occasion, you must take matters into your own hands. Do not hinge your path on the guidance of others. Carry your torch."

His mother's words flowed forth, a continuation of her guidance. "Should you desire a life shackled in servitude," she persisted, "persist in seeking the assistance of others. They may agree, yet the cost will become apparent. The decision rests entirely with you – it is your autonomy, your very life. They may fulfil your requests, but in return, you shall remain perpetually bound to them. Sacrificing your individuality for a meagre compensation, you reduce yourself to nought but an insignificant slave. Your identity slips through your grasp, leaving you bereft."

His mother articulated, "Anticipations resemble fragile glass. The firmer your grasp, the greater the likelihood of their shattering."

Shree Shambav expressed, "Pradeep, expectations breed reliance and reliance, in turn, begets the weight of burden or entanglement."

Shree Shambav conveyed, "Rely not on anything, for all shall depart in time. Ultimately, when the day closes, you shall find only yourself, and therein lies the ultimate truth."

Shree Shambav's smile lingered as he pressed onward, his voice a tapestry of contemplation and insight. "Pradeep," he began, his words unfolding with a gentle yet profound cadence, "there is a delicate paradox woven into the fabric of existence—a paradox that beckons us to ponder the nature of need and its transformation into burden. Imagine the thirsty soul, whose yearning for water is quenched, only to find himself burdened by the vessel that once held his relief. Picture the traveller, who, after the rain has ceased, carries an umbrella transformed from a shield to an encumbrance."

"A tree, once laden with the bounty of fruit, can evolve into a silent burden upon the earth when its giving has come to an end," he mused, a touch of melancholy woven into his tone. "And so it is, Pradeep," he continued, his words a delicate thread connecting the facets of life, "with the precious bonds of friendship. Once nurtured through moments of shared need, they, too, may turn into obligations once those needs have been met."

Shree Shambav's voice became deeper, conveying the weight of insight. "Imagine that when our desires are met, love itself may feel like a burden, its weight a testament to the depth of our attachments. Even the essence of our ancestors, our blood, may become a burden as material possessions are split among heirs."

He paused, allowing the gravity of his words to linger in the air, before delving more into the human experience. "Even knowledge gained from the pages of a book can become an anchor, a burden to bear, and wisdom imparted by a master, once a beacon of guidance, can, over time, become a gentle weight on our shoulders."

"In the autumn of life," Shree Shambav continued, "as the years accumulate, even the vessel that carries our consciousness—our body—can evolve into a burden, a reminder of the fleeting nature of existence itself." His voice held a feeling of acceptance, a recognition of life's cycles. "And so, Pradeep," he said softly, "even the act of supplication to the divine, once a fervent prayer, can become a burden as our needs are met."

Shree Shambav paused to let the weight of his words sink in, a pregnant pause before the conclusion. "Such is life's symphony, where desires fulfilled may lead to the orchestration of burdens carried. The ebb and flow of need and its metamorphosis resonate across the tapestry of our path."

Busy chasing

"The hues of attachment are painted on the canvas of human emotions, giving rise to desires that bloom like flowers. Yet, be wary, for beneath these cravings lie dormant seeds of rage, waiting for the right moment to sprout."

- *Shree Shambav*

Amid a discourse, a devotee named Kiran posed a question to the Master: "Master, what causes one to fall into the grip of attachment?"

With a serene smile, Shree Shambav responded, "The root of attachment is surprisingly uncomplicated. When we habitually dwell upon the idea that an object or a person holds happiness, it paves the way for attachment to take hold."

Shree Shambav expressed, "Whenever the mind becomes entangled in attachment, it opens the door to recurrent desires. And once desire takes root, it unfolds into two outcomes: the realisation of that desire or the sense of longing left unfulfilled."

Shree Shambav said, "Allow me to recount a captivating tale: In a forest dwelled a band of thieves, led by a merciless figure named Jagga. Their actions showed no compassion towards humanity, as they pillaged neighbouring villages. In due course, a twist of fate saw the birth of a son to Jagga and his wife. An unexpected transformation unfolded as Jagga, who was once heartless, found his heart softening through his deep affection for the child."

During a single night's slumber, he envisioned a haunting scenario—the King's soldiers had taken his life, leaving his son bereft. Upon awakening, he carried a lingering unease from the dream, but recognising its illusory nature, he regained his composure and resumed his daily responsibilities.

With the passage of years, Jagga's son, Darpan, posed a probing question: "Father, what drives us to plunder others?"

Amid hearty laughter shared among Jagga and his fellow robbers, he chimed in, "My dear son, it's the pursuit of money and riches."

Inquisitively, Darpan questioned, "Father, do we not possess ample wealth already?"

With a gentle smile, Jagga responded, "The greater your acquisitions, the stronger your desire to possess them becomes."

Curious, Darpan inquired, "Father, at what point do you envision yourself being content with your accumulation of wealth?"

Jagga's smile lingered as he replied, "That, my son, remains uncertain."

Leaving Darpan in the company of the other robbers, Jagga embarked on a mission to plunder the nearby village. As they journeyed through the forest's obscurity, a fleeting thought brushed Jagga's mind just before they entered the village's boundaries.

Jagga pondered within, "What propels my ongoing desire to plunder others?"

His contemplation deepened as he acknowledged, "I have amassed ample riches to secure the future of generations ahead, and yet, this insatiable hunger for wealth persists. How can I liberate myself from this relentless craving for money and riches?"

Drawing from his son's earlier conversation, Jagga recalled a conversation that held a semblance of truth.

Without delay, he instructed his comrades to abandon their plan of looting the village and instead return home. His fellow mates found themselves in an unfamiliar predicament, as their usual practice was to carry out their intended mission without deviation once a looting decision had been made.

Inquisitive voices arose from the group, as one of the robbers questioned the rationale behind their sudden change of plans. Jagga, however, urged a delay in the discussion, sensing that the present moment was not suitable for such deliberations. This prompted them to hasten their journey homeward.

The following morning, Jagga gathered his companions and posed thought-provoking questions: "What drives us to engage in plunder? Is it driven by hunger, our necessities, personal enjoyment, or the pursuit of extravagance?"

Jagga voiced, “Consider this—whatever we’ve seized through our raids, all stashed away beneath these rocks and within this cave. Has the accumulation of these material possessions truly altered our lives?”

A hushed contemplation fell upon the group until one of them finally inquired, “Then what course of action do you propose we take?”

Jagga admitted, “My certainty wavers; I’m devoid of an answer to this query.”

Perplexed, Jagga found himself grappling with the uncertainty regarding the next steps. While navigating the depths of the forest in solitude, he chanced upon a venerable sage seated beneath a tranquil tree, engrossed in serene meditation. The sage’s countenance radiated a serene glow, despite his ragged attire and visibly weakened state. In this paradoxical juxtaposition, the sage exuded an air of peace and contentment.

Jagga patiently awaited the sage’s awakening, and as the sage’s eyes gently opened, he lowered himself to the ground in a gesture of reverence. “I am Jagga, and I bear the weight of a dacoit’s deeds.”

The sage responded with a calm and composed demeanour, asking, “In what manner may I be of help to you?”

Jagga expressed with introspection, "Despite amassing riches that could suffice for generations ahead, I remain unfulfilled. What leads us to be ensnared by attachments?"

Continuing his contemplation, he acknowledged, "In my pursuit, I've caused harm to countless individuals. In mere hours, I've rendered them homeless, and for the allure of precious stones, metals, and currency, I've even taken lives."

A serene smile graced the sage's countenance as he responded, "Within each of us, diverse desires take root. The source of desire lies in the attachment cultivated by the mind. When the mind becomes entwined with an object or an individual, it births a recurring craving for that entity. Amid the contemplation of sensory objects, a bond forms between them and the mind, a connection that spawns attachment. This affinity nurtures attachment, which gives birth to desire, a flame that ignites the fire of anger."

The sage imparted, "Your deeds find their roots in your attachments."

Continuing, he added, "Frequently, our convictions align with the dictations of our mind, as we neglect the discernment between right and wrong. Often, the path of our desires remains unclear, leaving us uncertain about our true aspirations."

Jagga inquired, "Does the mind exert dominion over us?"

The sage responded, "The mind, which we seek to harness, guide, and steer toward our ultimate destination, possesses an intrinsic inclination to generate a multitude of desires. This tendency is akin to its default configuration—where certain desires prove advantageous, while others may be detrimental. Among these desires, some elevate our being, while others cast a shadow over our essence. The mind is a fountain of diverse desires, and this shared human experience envelops us all. It is our prerogative to diminish desires of lower nature and amplify those that propel us to loftier realms."

Jagga posed the question, "What characterises an upper-level desire?"

The sage responded, "By acquainting yourself with your essence and attuning to the voice of your inner consciousness, you shall glean insights into the verities that reside within."

Jagga inquired, "What defines a desire of lower nature?"

The sage replied, "In the realm of transgressions, an innate moral compass often plunges us into a sense of disquiet. Each of us is endowed with an innate yearning for righteousness and virtue. The voice of conscience emanates from the wellspring of goodness that resides within the soul. Thus, we cannot feign ignorance concerning the nature of actions like theft, deceit, slander, extortion, murder, tyranny, and corruption—they are all manifestations of malevolence. Despite our intuitive recognition of their inherent wrongness, we persist in these actions, seemingly impelled by a potent compulsion."

The sage carried on, "The influence of passion deceives the soul by fostering the notion that worldly possessions hold the key to contentment. Consequently, desires sprout for their acquisition. The fulfilment of such desires begets greed, while their frustration births anger. These emotional currents can lead individuals to commit transgressions."

Sage said, "Lust, your adversary, can be conquered through self-awareness. Once you grasp this truth, genuine happiness will be within your reach."

Shree Shambav remarked, "Kiran, all these intricacies have their roots in attachment. But what fuels attachment? People are attached to diverse aspects of life. Some become so engrossed in their pursuit of success that family life takes a backseat. Others hold their family so close that ambitions fade away. Some attach themselves to their businesses, while some tirelessly gather riches, and still others collect luxury items, each entangled in their sphere.

Shree Shambav's smile graced his lips as he conveyed, "We find ourselves engrossed in pursuits without truly comprehending what our heart truly desires."

The Nest of Unconditional Love

"In the tempest of life, a parent's sacrifice is a protective embrace, safeguarding their cherished ones."

– Shree Shambav

In a quaint village, time unfurled a story of an old man named Oliver. A heart adorned with the longing for his son, whom he hadn't seen for years. He yearned to reunite with his boy, who now resided in the vastness of a bustling city.

Oliver embarked on his journey, carrying his hopes and love in a simple bag. His steps took him to the city where his son had lived and worked.

At the place from which he once received cherished letters, Oliver knocked on the door, his eyes glistening with the anticipation of seeing his son. His heart, however, sank when someone other than his son answered.

He inquired, "I suppose James resides here?" the person replied, "No, he left this place long ago, years ago."

The news left Oliver disheartened. He wondered how he would find his son in this vast city.

As Oliver searched tirelessly, a stranger from afar approached him, asking, "Are you looking for James?" Oliver nodded in response.

"How do you know James?" Oliver questioned.

The stranger explained, "I used to work for him years ago."

Finally, Oliver got his son's current address, and with gratitude in his heart, he set forth with renewed hope.

Upon reaching the office where James worked, he inquired at the reception desk, "Could you please tell me where I can find James in this office?"

The receptionist, curious, inquired, "May I know your relation to him?"

With a kind smile, Oliver replied, "I'm his father."

Upon hearing this, the receptionist, in a moment of realisation, conveyed Oliver's presence to James, who was shocked and requested to meet his father immediately.

In James' office, as their eyes met, Oliver's welled with tears. A heartfelt reunion ensued as father and son engaged in simple conversation.

Touched by his father's visit, Oliver expressed his wife's desire to see their son. He asked, "Son, your mother yearns to see you. Can you come home with me?"

James hesitated, explaining, "I'm swamped with work on a crucial project, and my success depends on it. It's hard to manage a leave."

With a simple smile, Oliver replied, "You may carry on with your work, son. I'll return to our village this evening."

Yet, James, moved by his father's visit, asked him to stay a few days. Oliver, however, sensed his son's workload and declined, saying, "I don't wish to inconvenience you or become a burden. If there's another chance, I'd love to see you and your mother together."

Oliver left the city.

Days later, a strange dream haunted James. He dreamt of losing his parents and felt their suffering. He awoke in distress, reflecting on his ungrateful behaviour toward his father.

He immediately set off for the village, and as he approached, memories of his childhood, family, and hometown filled his thoughts.

Upon arriving at his childhood home, he discovered it abandoned. His parents were not there, and panic set in. Neighbours informed him of their new address, leading him to a deserted house in an eerily silent neighbourhood.

Oliver sat outside the empty house, waiting for his son's return. As James spotted his father from a distance, he began to run, tears streaming down his face. Father and son were reunited at last.

But James asked, "Father, where is Mother?"

Oliver, after a long silence, gently broke the news, "Your mother passed away a few days ago. She lastly hoped to see you."

James was in shock, and his tears flowed uncontrollably. "How are you, Father?" James asked, struggling to hold back his emotions. "What has led us to this point? We had wealth and riches."

Oliver smiled softly and replied, "I took a loan to pay for your education when you went to the city for college, and another for the car you wanted. Because of a loss in farming, I couldn't repay the loan, and we lost our home and farmland."

As the tears flowed down James' cheeks, Oliver continued, his voice quivering with the weight of his words, "I didn't want to burden you with our problems when I approached you for help. I just wished to fulfil your mother's last wish. So, I remained silent and let go of her last desire."

With a voice that trembled with regret, James whispered, "You should have told me. I'm not an outsider."

Turning to face James, his eyes filled with love and understanding, Oliver replied, "You were busy and stressed with work, my son, and I didn't want to add to your stress. We only wanted your happiness, and we believed we were doing the right thing."

Oliver then shared a story. "Let me narrate a story," he began, the tremors of emotion still clear in his voice.

Long ago, in the tranquil setting of a village, Kai sought wisdom from his revered guru, Silas, on the profound nature of a parent's love and sacrifice. Filled with curiosity, he asked, "Silas, how do you define a parent's love and sacrifice? What makes their love so special and their sacrifices so selfless?"

Silas, his eyes twinkling with the wisdom of years, was more than willing to illustrate this profound love. He wove a metaphorical tale, and with every word, the depth of parental love and sacrifice became clearer.

"Imagine, Kai," Silas began, "a little bird constructing its nest high up in a towering oak tree. The nest is its most precious possession, a haven where it lays its eggs and raises its young. The little bird nurtures its offspring with unwavering love, providing warmth, food, and protection. Day by day, it watches over them, teaching them to fly, to sing, and to thrive in the world."

Kai listened intently, captivated by the vivid imagery that was unfolding.

"But," Silas continued, "there comes a day when a fierce storm approaches, with winds that threaten to tear the little nest from the branches. The mother bird knows that her nest, her refuge, her entire world is at risk."

"In the face of the impending storm, she spreads her wings and hovers over her precious nest, shielding it from the raging tempest," Silas said. "She absorbs the brunt of the storm, the howling winds, the driving rain, the pelting hail, and the relentless lightning, all to ensure that her young ones remain safe within their shelter."

Kai's eyes widened with realisation, the depth of the metaphor striking a chord deep within his heart.

"Silas," Kai whispered, his voice brimming with emotion, "that's incredible. The mother bird's love is like a protective shield, and she sacrifices her well-being for her young."

Silas nodded with a knowing smile. "Indeed, Kai. A parent's love is a force of nature, a fierce and unyielding protector. Their sacrifices may go unnoticed, but they are enduring, profound, and unparalleled. It is in the warmth of their embrace, the sacrifices they make, and the nurturing care they provide that the essence of parental love and sacrifice truly shines."

Kai sat in silence, his heart heavy with the weight of this newfound understanding. He realised that the bond between parents and their children was indeed a treasure beyond measure, a love as deep and enduring as the roots of the oak tree and as powerful as the winds of a storm.

With these lessons etched in his heart, James couldn't hold back his tears any longer. He embraced his father tightly, apologising for his past actions, and expressing a love that had found its way back into his heart.

Oliver smiled warmly and said, "No need for apologies, my son. I'm content with what I have now. The only expectation parents have is to spend time with their children, especially in their old age. I understand that travelling to visit a child can be challenging."

With tears glistening in their eyes, father and son found forgiveness and reconciliation. They cherished the moments they had together, knowing that the bonds of love and family were stronger than any trials they had faced.

You are never alone

"Journey will reveal a profound wisdom: the relentless pursuit and ceaseless quest for perfection need not define your existence. Instead, you possess the freedom to merely exist — to wholly embrace your unrefined essence and find solace in the simple act of being present in this very moment."

- *Shree Shambav*

On a particular occasion, Shree Shambav embarked on a journey accompanied by his devoted disciple, Veda. Their path led them through the enigmatic depths of a dense forest, where towering trees and verdant foliage enveloped them. Amidst the dimly lit and secluded environment, Veda found himself slightly unsettled as he observed the obscure surroundings.

In his mind, Veda pondered, "The darkness envelops us, and the chill lingers in the air. We must hasten our pace. An uncanny sensation grips me—I feel as though I'm being pursued, an intuition born from my experiences. Beads of sweat formed on my forehead, triggered by a mixture of fear and urgency. Amid the obscurity of the woods, I struggled with desperation to find my way forward. My thoughts were a jumbled mess. Each sound I heard seemed to heighten my unease. The thick canopy of leaves obscured my vision, allowing only a faint view a few meters in any direction. Yet, I knew I couldn't refuse my master's guidance. The ground beneath me, softened by the previous night's rain, clung to my feet, creating a sensation akin to being glued in place."

Shambav conveyed, "Veda, initially, you might feel a touch of unease as we venture through the jungle at night. We'll tread along the obscure path, guided by unseen forces, walking without the aid of light. Gradually, our vision will attune to a fresh perspective, revealing a world that awakens as the creatures of the night slumber. As some creatures rest, others rouse to begin their nocturnal activities."

Embarking on a nighttime expedition through the jungle offers us an unparalleled chance to experience and witness the enchanting nocturnal marvels that the forest conceals. Amid the profound obscurity of the woods, we'll immerse ourselves in the symphony of countless insect melodies, and we might find ourselves suddenly enveloped by curious creatures of the night, evading the gaze of their daytime predators. We may encounter an array of beings: tree frogs, an assortment of insects, diverse spider species, and even reptiles. Nocturnal monkeys, armadillos, and ethereal moths also come to life as the sun sets.

Veda inquired, "Master, is it necessary for us to journey through these hours of darkness? Could we not find respite beneath this tree until the first light of dawn?"

With a smile, the Master responded, "Veda, let go of your concerns. These woods possess an enchanting power that often defies belief. The forest welcomes you with open arms, devoid of judgment, offering strength and solace. It envelops you with its captivating beauty, sounds, and scents, and it safeguards you. Have faith in its embrace."

Veda silently contemplated, "No matter what, I must accompany the Master. Though his heart raced with apprehension, he couldn't defy his master's wishes."

A twig snapping echoed through the air, causing Veda to halt abruptly. He spun around, his gaze darting anxiously in search of the source, but the dim illumination offered little clarity. Almost in an instant, a distant thunderous sound reverberated, prompting an involuntary cry of fear from Veda. His body trembled, and he stood on the precipice of bolting further into the heart of the woods.

Shambav reassured, "Veda, let go of your worries. I assure you, you'll find joy in this journey."

Veda replied, "Master, I still hold the preference of travelling when the sun has illuminated the surroundings."

Shambav chuckled and remarked, "Veda, entering a forest is an invigorating experience. Crossing its threshold is akin to passing through a gateway. As you step in, you shed all the chaos, apprehensions, and concerns. Instead, you're welcomed by tranquillity, the sweet aroma of nature, and a heightened feeling of aliveness."

Veda found himself ensnared in a tangle of branches as if they conspired to strike him from every direction. His thoughts echoed with fervent prayers for his safety, aching for the sun's emergence. His breath came in ragged gasps, his heart pounding like a wild drumbeat. Nervousness clung to him, mingling with the sheen of sweat on his skin. The abyss of darkness enveloped him, and his surroundings took on a muted hue. His mind spiralled with various unsettling scenarios: the prospect of encountering venomous insects or lurking reptiles, the fear of stumbling and causing harm, and the gnawing worry of losing his way in the impenetrable forest. Amidst Veda's turmoil, Shambav sensed his apprehension...

Shambav's voice resonated gently, "Veda, a path through the woods beckons you to venture deeper into the very soul of the forest. With each step, the worries that plagued your mind, the fears that clenched your heart, the urgency that governs your days, and the responsibilities that burden your existence will fade into oblivion. This journey will unveil the wisdom that you need not continuously strive, nor perpetually chase perfection. You have the liberty to simply be — to embrace your raw essence and be present in this moment."

Shambav's voice carried a serene assurance, "Veda, as you tread on, your body naturally eases into a state of restfulness. Each breath flows with an effortless depth, embracing you in its soothing rhythm. With every inhalation, a renewed sense of wellness and vitality permeates your being. The symphony of fragrances envelopes you, its beauty defying description. In this moment, the act of breathing may even grant you the sensation of experiencing life anew, as if for the very first time."

Veda swiftly regained his composure, his vision adapting to the surrounding obscurity, and a newfound sense of ease enveloped him.

With newfound confidence, he remarked, "Indeed, Master, I sense a transformation within me. I feel a newfound strength coursing through my being."

Veda said, "The forest air carries a peculiar yet invigorating fragrance. It mingles scents of moist moss, rain-soaked tree bark, blossoms, pine-laden trails, and an underlying hint of imminent adventure."

Shambav grinned and remarked, "Staying here for a few months can do wonders for one's mental well-being and serve as a source of rejuvenation."

Shambav exclaimed, "Veda, can you hear it? The symphony of creatures fills the night with their unique sounds. Each one has a purpose, whether it's to attract a mate, search for food, or ward off potential threats. These nocturnal beings, spanning from tiny insects to graceful birds and stealthy mammals, inhabit every corner of this forest. It's simply astonishing, isn't it?"

Veda grinned and expressed, "Master, your ability to find value in everything is truly remarkable. I'm constantly amazed by your profound knowledge."

After an extensive walk through the dense forest, they decided to take a brief respite, settling on a large stone. It was then that they began to witness the gentle rays of sunlight filtering through the trees, gradually illuminating the forest around them.

Veda exclaimed, "Look, we're finally seeing some rays breaking through."

Shambav responded, "Veda, the forest's sunlight creates a mesmerising interplay of shadows and colours amidst the trees. It can feel warm or cool, gloomy or bright, but when observed with a peaceful heart, it remains a safe, familiar, and beautiful sight. As you explore the forest's intricate wonders with dedication, you'll find that time becomes irrelevant in this world of the woods."

Veda acknowledged, "You're right, Master."

Following a brief rest and enjoying some available fruits, they resumed their journey.

Shambav remarked, "The forest not only sustains us but also nurtures our future generations."

Veda's curiosity drove him to inquire, "Master, how does it look after us?"

Shambav explained, "It has a preventive effect against allergies, strengthening us by exposing us to beneficial bacteria. We acquire them by regularly immersing ourselves in nature, starting from a young age."

Shambav explained, "Trees enhance aesthetics and enhance our well-being. They mitigate pollution, conserve water, and prevent soil erosion. They influence the local climate and reduce noise pollution while promoting plant and animal diversity."

Continuing, Shambav emphasised, "The impact of proximity to nature can be profoundly positive. Even the youngest child introduced to nature and biodiversity may develop a deep fascination for birds, butterflies, or insects, sparking endless excitement."

Veda inquired, "Master, are you suggesting that growing up close to nature from a young age is beneficial?"

Shambav affirmed, "Indeed if we have the opportunity to be surrounded by nature in our formative years, it leaves an indelibly positive imprint that lasts a lifetime. Being amidst trees instils a sense of safety. The forest serves as a sanctuary, a space for reprieve. It quiets the constant chatter of thoughts and allows us to appreciate the simple joys, helping us discern what truly matters."

Shambav continued, "The eyes can finally find solace as well. Your vision is no longer assailed by the harsh glare of bright lights, gleaming surfaces, or the imposing structures of man's creation. You can allow your eyes to relax by gazing into the depths of the forest or up into the canopy of leaves. Nature, despite all the intricacies crafted by Mother Earth, exudes an impeccable and soothing beauty."

Soon, Veda noticed some moss-covered tree trunks and reached out to touch them, prompting him to inquire about his master about the moss.

Shambav said, "Bountiful clumps of moss beckon you to reach out and touch them, as do the tree trunks, rocks, and every other natural element you encounter along this path. Plunge your hand into the moss and experience the cool, fragrant earth. Press your ear to the weathered trunk of a fallen tree, and you'll receive insights far surpassing the wisdom of even the most learned human."

Veda smiled and responded, "Indeed, Master."

Shambav expressed, "The forest serves as a reminder of our true essence and our origins."

Shambav elaborated, “It heals us through all our senses. Our eyes find solace in the embrace of nature’s beauty; our ears are granted moments of profound silence, allowing us to tune into the harmonious melodies of the natural world. We can connect with nature through touch, whether it’s with our hands, feet, or even our cheekbones. And within our noses, we encounter the wondrous fragrances of the earth, trees, water, and rocks, each scent vividly shifting with the weather and seasons.”

Veda plucked a handful of berries and savoured their freshness, remarking, “These berries are truly delightful.”

Shambav inquired, “Veda, have you ever observed how, like various creatures, both big and small, we, too, relish the sweetness of berries?”

Veda directed his master’s attention, saying, “Master, behold this exquisite lake.”

Shambav suggested, “Let’s make our way to the water’s edge,” and they settled into a few moments of profound stillness.

Shambav encouraged, “Listen to the ripples, perceive their fragrance, and let them convey their message to you.”

Veda gently shut his eyes, attentively heeding his master's counsel.

Veda approached the lakeshore, knelt, and carefully scooped water into his hands. As he sipped the cool liquid, his reflection in the water caught his eye, and he began to appreciate the enchanting surroundings of the forest.

Shambav interjected, "Allow me to share a story," he continued. "Once, a wise man named Shankara was strolling through the fields when he encountered a troubled young man named Lalit."

Shankara remarked, "Lalit, on such a splendid day, it's quite a challenge to maintain such a solemn demeanour."

Lalit, intrigued by Shankara's comment, began to observe his surroundings more attentively. His gaze swept across the landscape, but nothing appeared to captivate his attention. Despite his keen observation, he struggled to find anything that piqued his interest.

After a prolonged silence, Lalith confessed, "I'm uncertain; nothing seems to hold my interest."

Shankara wore a serene smile as he strolled along the periphery of a tranquil pond, surrounded by towering trees and a ground blanketed in dry leaves. The atmosphere remained utterly serene and hushed.

Shankara gently suggested, “Lalit, please take a seat.”

Lalit examined the ground attentively, brushing away any debris before settling down.

Shankar directed his attention, saying, “Observe this serene, motionless water.”

Lalit gazed carefully at the tranquil water, nodding in acknowledgement.

Shankar instructed, “Now, locate a little pebble.”

Lalith inquired, “A small pebble?”

Shankar smiled and confirmed, “Yes, Lalit, find a small pebble and toss it into the pond.”

Lalit scanned his surroundings, located a pebble, and hurled it as far as he could.

Shankar inquired, “Lalit, can you describe what you observe?”

Lalit, focusing intently on catching every nuance, gazed at the water’s surface.

Lalit replied, “I see ripples.”

Shankar followed up, "Lalit, where did these ripples originate?"

Lalit responded, "They came from the pebble I tossed into the pond, Master."

Shankar, his tone serious, instructed, "Now, reach your hand into the water and try to still the ripples."

Lalit, puzzled and uncertain, dipped his hand into the water, attempting to halt the ripples. However, his actions only seemed to create more ripples, leaving the young man thoroughly perplexed.

Lalit's mind swirled with questions. Where was this lesson leading? Had he made an error in seeking the Master? Maybe, as he was not a formal student, the Master wouldn't assist him. A barrage of thoughts raced through his head, leaving him puzzled as he waited without further inquiries.

Shankar eventually asked, "Lalit, were you successful in stilling the ripples with your hands?"

Lalit responded, "No, of course not. Could you have stopped the ripples, then?"

Lalit said, "No, Master."

Shankar said, “I only caused more ripples. What if you had stopped the pebble from entering the water to begin with?”

Shankar chuckled heartily, and this time, Lalit didn’t feel disheartened; he sensed there was a profound message in his Master’s words.

Shankar went on, “Young man, don’t let frustration consume you. When you find yourself unhappy with your life, intercept the stone before it touches the water. Instead of dwelling on undoing your actions, focus on changing your course before you act.”

The Master regarded the young man with a gentle expression. Lalit’s curiosity led him to inquire, “Master, how can I possibly know what I’m going to do before I do it?”

Shankar responded, “Accept the responsibility for crafting your own life. When dealing with a doctor to address an ailment, inquire about the root cause of the illness. Don’t merely address the surface issues; keep seeking answers.”

Lalit’s face lit up with a smile, and he inquired, “Master, so you mean to say that I already possess the answers I seek?”

Shankar clarified, "You may not hold those answers at this moment, but by posing the right questions, you will uncover the answers you're searching for."

Lalit inquired, "Master, what defines the 'right' questions? Aren't all questions valuable in their way?"

Shankar imparted his wisdom, saying, "Indeed, there are no 'wrong' questions, only those left unasked. Asking is the key, for answers come to those who seek them. However, it's your responsibility to initiate the inquiry. No one else can do it on your behalf."

As Veda listened to the story, he found himself immersed in the memories of his journey through the dark forest, contemplating the source of his fears and anxieties and how he had managed to overcome them.

Shambav marvelled, "Listen to the melodic symphony of water! Whether it's the vibrant babble of a forest brook, the serenity of a pond, the expanse of a lake, or the power of a grand river, it forms a unique world right by your side, offering respite to your mind, rejuvenating your spirit."

Shambav continued, "Have you ever wondered about the hidden world beneath the water's surface? The playful gurgle and spirited flow create a sense of completeness – a view you could savour indefinitely. The water exudes a fresh, invigorating scent, brimming with an energy you can readily absorb. That's why spending time by the waterfront always feels so invigorating."

Veda remarked, "In the forest, solitude is a foreign concept. You're never truly alone. There's a multitude of wanderers here: some large, some small, some winged, others furry, fluttering, or crawling."

Shambav added, "If you observe closely, you'll see a tapestry of life unfolding. A flock of birds engages in playful banter, an army of ants diligently prepares for inclement weather, and butterflies and bees flutter about, busy with their vital pollination work. The birds are animated, almost as if they're conversing with you. Look downwards, beneath mushrooms, into crevices between rocks, or at the intricate network of tree roots. Pay attention to even the tiniest creatures, treating them with the respect they deserve, for in the forest, we are all equals. Each beetle, snail, and frog holds a unique and irreplaceable role. Many beings and elements can offer guidance. All that's required is a clear vision and an open mind."

Shambav remarked, "The forest extends its gentle touch, rejuvenating all who venture into its embrace, even those who may not hold it dear. Yet, those who cherish and love it will receive greater rewards than they can fathom."

Shambav continued, "When the sun retreats, the forest transforms, becoming a realm of mysteries inhabited by some of Earth's most enigmatic life forms. If you've only witnessed the jungle during the daylight hours, you've merely glimpsed half of its wondrous paradise. This is why we embarked on a part of our journey in the darkness — to truly comprehend the forest in its entirety."

Veda, reflecting on these words, said, "Master, I've come to realise the profound truth…"

Life is a mirror

"Life serves as a mirror; what you offer, you shall receive in kind. The seeds you sow determine your harvest. The reflections you observe in others are but echoes of yourself."

– Shree Shambav

During their journey through the hills, Shree Shambav and his disciples encountered a serene, flowing stream. Shree Shambav, sensing the need for a brief respite, took a short break. As the devotees refreshed themselves with the crisp, cool water, their attention was drawn to a man seated by the stream, his countenance steeped in sadness and contemplation.

After quenching their thirst and finding a shady spot beneath a tree to rest, one of the devotees, named Padma, couldn't help but feel compassion for the solitary man sitting alongside the stream.

Padma approached the despondent man and gently inquired, "It appears you've been here by the stream for quite some time, and your countenance reflects deep unhappiness."

The man, Manjunath, sighed heavily and replied, "I am utterly alone; no one has faith in me. This life has become an overwhelming burden, and I'm uncertain how much longer I must bear it."

Padma offered words of solace to Manjunath and then guided him to where Shree Shambav was seated.

Padma inquired, "Where did things take a turn for the worse?"

Manjunath shared, "My wife would always stress that robbing and causing harm to others was an improper way to live. She urged me to work diligently to provide for ourselves and our only child. I, however, ignored her wise counsel, and the years passed. People in the neighbouring village grew weary of my thieving and turmoil."

Manjunath's eyes filled with tears as he continued, "Someone from the nearby village set our house ablaze, reducing it to ashes. In this tragic event, I lost both my wife and child. For a few years, I sustained myself with what little savings remained and constructed this modest dwelling."

Shree Shambav attentively listened to Manjunath's concerns; his eyes gently closed in contemplation.

Manjunath continued, "I once yearned for revenge against the person who had set fire to my family and my home. My anger consumed me, and I tirelessly searched for this individual for years. Then, one day, I had a dream. A voice spoke, saying, 'As you sow, so shall you reap. You initiated harm and robbery, causing suffering to others, and ultimately, you lost your family and happiness. Your anger blinds you. Consider being the good person your wife always wanted you to be.'"

Manjunath further explained, "After hearing this message, I began to question my actions. Why was I living in solitude? I had wronged innocent and hardworking people. It was then that I decided to toil diligently to earn my livelihood."

Padma inquired, "That sounds commendable. Then what is the source of your sadness?"

Manjunath replied, "I have dedicated myself to hard work. Every year, I yield three harvests from my land, reserving one portion for my sustenance and distributing the rest to the nearby villages. Yet, nobody truly accepts me, and they rarely engage in genuine conversation."

He continued, "People around here only wear smiles and converse out of fear, not out of respect. Despite my repeated assurances that I have changed, that I am no longer the person who once caused harm and robbed them."

Manjunath expressed his loneliness, saying, "Living in solitude has made my life melancholic. Despite my diligent efforts, I have no one to share my moments of joy and happiness with."

Shree Shambav wore a gentle smile as he spoke. "When you plant rice, your harvest will yield rice. When you plant vegetables, you'll gather vegetables. If you extend love to others, there's a chance they might reciprocate. However, if you engage in harmful actions toward others, you'll ultimately receive harm in return. It's a principle: a person reaps what they sow."

Continuing, Shree Shambav said, "One's life is akin to a mirror, reflecting the actions they have taken or are yet to take. Thus, misdeeds yield misfortune, while virtuous actions bring about goodness. By engaging in positive actions, we can invite better times. However, these actions cannot erase the consequences of our past misdeeds; we must still face their repercussions. We are bound by this cycle of duality, unable to break free. But by sowing the right seeds, by engaging in righteous actions, we can hope to escape this cycle's clutches."

Shree Shambav began a story, saying, "Once, in a quaint village, there resided two grain merchants, Rakesh and Roshan. In those bygone days, folks used large earthen pots with openings at both the top and bottom to store their grains."

Shree Shambav continued, "Rakesh offered high-quality rice grains, while Roshan dealt in lower-quality rice. Rakesh quickly gained the admiration of the villagers, both for the superior quality of his rice and for the reasonable prices he offered. Consequently, Rakesh's reputation and wealth grew, earning him respect and prominence in the community."

Because of his inferior-quality rice, people gradually began to shy away from purchasing from Roshan. Recognising his mistake, he was filled with regret and resolved to offer high-quality rice at an exceptionally fair price. Despite his genuine intentions, he found people remained uninterested.

In the meantime, Rakesh's avarice grew, causing him to resort to selling inferior-quality rice. Strangely, customers continued to purchase from him.

This left Roshan puzzled. Why were they still choosing to buy from Rakesh?

Rakesh soon came to the realisation that he needed to empty the earthen pot of the inferior-quality rice before offering the superior-quality grains.

Conversely, Roshan understood that the earthen pot must be emptied of the superior-quality rice before serving the inferior-quality grains.

Shree Shambav conveyed, "Manjunath, your current actions of providing sustenance and care to those in need are commendable. They accumulate as good deeds, yet they cannot erase your past actions."

He continued with a smile, "Life acts as a mirror, reflecting to us what we offer. Just as we sow, so shall we reap. The way we perceive others is often a reflection of ourselves."

True Friendship

"A true friend is the cornerstone of a life built on the bedrock of shared values, offering a hand to hold in today's storms and a beacon of hope for tomorrow's horizons."

– Shree Shambav

In a discourse, a devoted follower by the name of Roopa posed a question, asking, "Master, how can one distinguish true friendship?"

Shree Shambav replied, "Friendship is a connection of mutual affection between individuals or living beings. Although this definition appears straightforward, the reality of friendship can be intricate. True friendships are a rare and precious gem, while false friends can be detrimental and should be steered clear of. Yet discerning the line between authentic and counterfeit friendship is not always an easy task."

Roopa inquired further, "Master, how can we discern between genuine and insincere friendships?"

Shree Shambav responded with a gentle smile, "People often seek connections with others for various motives. Sometimes, shared interests serve as the foundation. In other instances, external factors like wealth, power, or influence may drive individuals to form friendships. Typically, true friendships prove to be enduring, standing the test of time, while counterfeit ones tend to disintegrate or conclude on a sour note."

Shree Shambav explained, "A genuine friendship doesn't rely on utility or momentary pleasure but thrives on mutual respect, admiration, and appreciation for the other person. This kind of friendship develops and strengthens over time.

Relationships built on the fleeting aspects of utility or pleasure tend to be fragile and are often short-lived. Consider how many connections falter before truly beginning because they are founded on the transient nature of utility or pleasure."

Shree Shambav continued, "A true friendship finds its roots in shared principles and virtues. It's the type of friendship that can grow even stronger as time passes."

Roopa inquired, "So, what defines a true friend?"

Shree Shambav replied, "A genuine friend is someone who staunchly supports you. When others attempt to harm you emotionally or physically, they go to great lengths to ensure your safety. They don't consider who is trying to hurt you; they will defend you under any circumstances wherever and whenever needed. If they can assist you, they'll do so selflessly and without expecting anything in return. A true friend is not someone who constantly relays negative things that others say about you. Firstly, they make their stance clear through both their words and actions, demonstrating where they stand about you. Secondly, they do not passively stand by when others are disparaging you, no matter the potential social consequences they may face. A true friend is there for you both when it's convenient and when it's not. They remain steadfastly by your side, whether you are present or absent."

Shree Shambav conveyed, "A true friend responds to you with empathy, candour, reliability, mutual respect, and a broader perspective. They uphold honesty when it truly counts, without attempting to deceive you to appear stronger, more successful, or superior. Authentic friendships require a degree of vulnerability. When a friend confides in you, revealing their struggles and disappointments, it underscores the trust and significance they assign to your relationship."

"A genuine friend doesn't limit their honesty to themselves; they extend it to you as well," he continued. They are competent in participating in uncomfortable conversations and addressing issues that you may not want to hear. The important thing is that they do it with love and tact. A good friend does not tear you down; instead, they hold you to a standard they believe your character deserves."

Shree Shambav expressed, "We shouldn't seek a friend who adapts to your changes, or simply follows your lead, as your own shadow does that job effectively."

He continued, "Allow me to share a lovely story from days gone by. Once upon a time, there resided a Macaw by the name of Olivia. She made her home on an ancient fig tree, where she relished the ripe fruits it offered, living a contented life."

After several years, the fig tree aged and ceased producing any fruit. Despite this, Olivia was steadfast in her decision not to depart as her other companions had done.

The fig tree implored, "Olivia, the time has come for you to depart from me and seek a new abode. I have grown old and can no longer bear fruit. If you remain here, you will face starvation."

Olivia replied, "You are not just a friend to me; you are the embodiment of my well-wishes. When my parents passed away when I was very young, you were there to care for me. You've imparted valuable lessons on empathy, honesty, and kindness to others. I cannot abandon you. I am willing to stay by your side, even if it means I might meet my end here."

The fig tree was deeply concerned and unsure of how to persuade Olivia. She worried that Olivia might perish due to hunger if she didn't depart and seek sustenance elsewhere.

The fig tree gently spoke, "Olivia, it's time for you to depart. You are braver than you may realise, stronger than you appear, and smarter than you think. Please remember, even if we are physically apart, my presence will always be with you."

Tears welled up in Olivia's eyes as she replied, "Why should I abandon you in your old age? You've cared for my parents, my grandparents. How can I leave you when you are frail? How can I seek happiness elsewhere without your company? If it pleases the divine for me to meet my end here, I accept it willingly."

The fig tree felt disheartened; her attempts to persuade Olivia had been in vain. Offering comfort, she embraced Olivia, and after some time, they both drifted into slumber.

Suddenly, a loud noise and a brilliant light startled them awake. They heard a voice addressing Olivia, "Why have you not departed from this tree? It can no longer bear fruit. If you persist, you will meet your demise."

Olivia replied, "Lord, I cannot abandon my friend, who has nourished me for countless years."

The voice responded, "Olivia, I am moved by your genuine friendship and your deep affection for the tree. What is your wish?"

Olivia humbly lowered her head and requested, "Lord, please bless my friend with the ability to bear fruit throughout the year, just as it did in the past."

The voice granted her request, and the fig tree rejuvenated, laden with fruits. Overwhelmed with emotion, Olivia bowed in gratitude, tears streaming down her cheeks. The voice vanished, bestowing blessings upon both of them.

Shree Shambav remarked, "Roopa, you tend to draw towards you what reflects your essence."

He went on, "Many of us seem to gravitate towards negative individuals in our lives. These might include friends with hidden agendas, narcissistic companions, or those with questionable intentions."

Every individual tends to attract people who share their innermost convictions in some way. This does not suggest that people attract carbon duplicates of themselves, but rather people and relationships who share their core ideals. A person who emanates confidence, self-assurance, and contentment, for example, is likely to attract supportive companions who raise them. Those with low self-esteem, unresolved difficulties, and limited confidence, on the other hand, are more likely to attract unfavourable friendships. This can lead to a cyclical trend because the company one keeps has a considerable impact on one's self-perception and worldview.

Shree Shambav emphasised, "Transforming one's self-perception can yield remarkable results. A genuine friend stands by your side during traumas, disappointments, and even mental health struggles. They won't abandon you when it's more convenient to do so. A true friend remains steadfast in both your failures and successes. They grant you the freedom to be your authentic self and to experience your emotions fully. They defend and protect you, regardless of who may threaten you. Their honesty shines brightest when it's needed most."

Shree Shambav concluded by saying, "Roopa, in this world, there are a few precious things, and true friendship is undoubtedly one of them."

You changed my life

"Only in the gentle embrace of parenthood do we uncover the hidden treasures of our own parents' sacrifices, and in the echoes of our children's laughter, we find the bittersweet symphony of our upbringing."

– Shree Shambav

While traversing through the village, an elderly gentleman named Daksh noticed a crowd gathered around a house. Intrigued, he decided to pause and investigate the commotion.

Daksh inquired, "What is the reason for all this commotion and confusion?"

A person named Purab, who stood nearby, remarked, "It's unfortunate that the elderly parents are being mistreated and harassed by their son."

Daksh remained silent for a moment before posing the question, "What could be the reason for his behaviour?"

Purab explained, "They were a prosperous family and had just one son. They raised him with abundant love and care. Initially, he was a well-behaved child, but after falling in with a bad crowd, he began tormenting his parents. At first, it was just shouting and causing trouble, but now it has escalated to physical abuse."

Daksh inquired, "Why haven't the parents taken any action despite facing all this trouble?"

Purab remarked, "They still love him unconditionally..."

Daksh fell silent for several minutes, then he moved away from the scene. The incident troubled him deeply, and he spent the entire night reflecting on it.

The following morning, he returned to the same location and waited beneath a tree for a few hours. Before long, he observed a man emerging from the house.

Daksh introduced himself to the man and inquired about his name. The other individual, Tejas, revealed his identity. Curiously, Daksh inquired, "Tejas, what is the reason for your aversion to your parents?"

Tejas expressed, "Daksh, they lack understanding in many aspects of my life. They scrutinise all my actions, expenses, and my every move."

Tejas continued, "To prevent them from doing this incessantly, I resort to issuing threats and occasionally causing them some distress."

Daksh inquired, "Do you not experience sorrow when they are in pain?"

Tejas offered a smile and replied, "I feel as though I've exhausted all the other alternatives."

Daksh then proposed, "May I share a story with you?"

Tejas smiled and responded, "I'm not particularly fond of hearing stories, but if you insist, I'll make an effort to listen."

Daksh replied, "That's very gracious of you."

Daksh then began his tale, saying, "A long time ago, there lived a couple named Yuvraj and Charvi. They were a content and highly empathetic pair. However, despite the passing of many years, they remained childless."

One day, Yuvraj inquired, "Charvi, you've been feeling discontented lately."

Charvi responded, "Indeed, Yuvraj. We've led a virtuous life, showing kindness to all living beings, and never succumbed to greed or jealousy. Yet, why hasn't the Supreme blessed us with children?"

Yuvraj wore a smile and gently remarked, "Charvi, whatever the Supreme does, He does it with a purpose."

Charvi expressed, "I find it challenging to perceive things as positively as you do. Each passing day, guilt and unhappiness seem to consume me."

Yuvraj suggested, "Charvi, perhaps we should invest more time with trees, plants, and other living beings. It might aid you in overcoming these thoughts."

Although Charvi remained unconvinced, she chose to remain silent.

A few days later, they journeyed to a nearby town to partake in a wedding celebration. As they were engrossed in the festivities at a distance, they noticed a child sitting alone, sobbing, and clad in tattered clothing. There was no one attending to his needs.

Yuvraj inquired, "One of his friends, gesturing toward the child, asked why that child had been left unattended with no one to care for him."

Yuvraj's friend explained, "The child is an orphan, and some of his relatives handle his care. Unfortunately, they perceive him as a burden because of their impoverished circumstances."

Upon overhearing this conversation, Charvi beckoned to Yuvraj and inquired, "Why don't we consider looking after this child?"

Yuvraj suggested, "Charvi, perhaps we should allow some time for contemplation before making a decision. Your longing for a child is urging you, and we should carefully consider our choice."

Charvi responded firmly, "Yuvraj, my prayers have illuminated a path for me. I don't wish to let this opportunity slip away."

Despite Yuvraj's attempts to persuade Charvi, she remained steadfast in her determination to adopt the child.

Yuvraj expressed, "Charvi, my greatest desire is to see you happy. If having that child brings you happiness, please proceed."

Subsequently, Yuvraj and his friend held conversations with their relatives regarding the child's adoption, and they decided to welcome him into their family.

Charvi became engrossed in caring for and playing with the child, whom they named Advik. Yuvraj also developed a strong bond with Advik, and they shared many joyous moments.

The child matured and began attending a local school after gaining admission. During his early years, he displayed a strong attachment to his parents, but as he got older, he gradually fell in with a negative crowd.

At the outset, he began deceiving his parents, prompting Yuvraj to caution Charvi that their son was heading down the wrong path. However, Charvi consistently stood by her son, reassuring Yuvraj, "He's still a child; he will find his way, eventually."

Gradually, Advik progressed from lying to stealing money, which left Yuvraj discontented. He confided in Charvi, expressing his concern that the situation was deteriorating and that they needed to intervene.

Despite Yuvraj's warning, Charvi chose to disregard his words. Her deep affection for their child remained unaffected, and she did not try to impart a sense of right and wrong to him.

As time passed, Advik developed a consistent habit of stealing both objects and money, while Charvi continued to turn a blind eye because of her overwhelming love for her child.

Yuvraj, growing increasingly unhappy with the unfolding events, began distancing himself from Charvi and refrained from offering advice to their child.

He didn't limit himself to just stealing money and possessions; he embraced a range of detrimental habits. At this point, Charvi came to recognise her past errors and made sincere efforts to educate her child about the concepts of right and wrong. She also took the opportunity to explain to him why Yuvraj hadn't spoken to her for the past seven years and why he seemed upset with their son.

The young child chuckled and responded, "Why should I be concerned if my father isn't talking to me? My only concern is you. He was never a good father; he was always finding fault with me." With those words, he departed.

Charvi found herself uncertain about her next course of action. After much contemplation, she eventually spoke, saying, "Yuvraj, I've attempted to persuade our child, but he refuses to heed my advice. How can I bring him back to the way he was when he was younger?"

Yuvraj responded, "Charvi, we must prevent issues from taking root in the first place. You allowed them to take root, and now he is inadvertently causing pain to both us and himself."

Yuvraj added, "We should address the situation, but let's not rush into it. We must approach him with understanding and compassion."

Tears welled up in Charvi's eyes, and she uttered, "Yuvraj, he's my son, and I can't bear to lose him."

Yuvraj remained silent, lowering his head in response.

Before long, they were startled by a loud thud on the door. With a heavy heart, Charvi approached and unlocked it, only to discover her son, heavily intoxicated and struggling to maintain his balance. He somehow managed to make his way to his room.

Witnessing her son's condition, Charvi couldn't bear it any longer. She entered her son's room and inquired, "Do you realise what you're doing?"

Advik retorted, "Mother, will you please stay quiet?"

Charvi became distressed, and in the midst of her upset, Yuvraj hurried over and advised, "We should discuss this with him in the morning."

Advik chimed in, "Mother, pay attention to the wisdom of the old man. He's the right one to offer advice."

The following morning, Advik asked his mother for money, but Charvi adamantly declined, not giving him a single penny.

As usual, Advik stated, "You two are terrible parents. I was born in the wrong place, and I despise being in this house. I can't stand my father's face, and I loathe every word he says."

Upon hearing this, Charvi couldn't contain her anger any longer and erupted, "You're correct, we are not good parents because we are not your parents."

Advik inquired, "What?"

Charvi replied, "Listen, allow me to speak the truth for once. I've endured your words for years. Yes, you were born in the wrong place because you seem to have no idea where that place even is."

Advik exclaimed, "You're testing my patience."

Charvi remarked, "Please, hear the complete truth. You may indeed grow to dislike this home because when nobody else was there to care for you, we showered you with unconditional love and provided you with the utmost comfort. Now, when it's your turn to reciprocate, you're doing so in the least appropriate manner."

Charvi stated, "You may come to dislike your father, detest his words, and use derogatory terms like 'old man' and more. However, he remains silent not because he's hurt by it, but to spare you from feeling upset."

Yuvraj made every effort to prevent Charvi from continuing to speak.

Charvi expressed, "If you were truly my son, I believe you would not have conducted yourself in this manner."

In an instant, Charvi found herself on the floor, blood trickling from her head. Yuvraj hurriedly tried to rouse her, but she remained unresponsive.

Yuvraj rushed her to the hospital, but it was futile as she had already passed away.

Yuvraj inquired of his son, "Do you comprehend the impact of your actions on your mother, who cherished you above all else in this world? Have you ever contemplated what you've forfeited because of your anger?"

Yuvraj went on, "Your destructive habits have consumed you. I have lost a wonderful partner. All I can implore is for you to treat others kindly, my child."

Before long, Advik discovered that his father had passed away. Later on, Advik received a jail sentence of several years.

Daksh, tearful and distraught, commented, "Due to a single action by Advik – pushing his mother – the entire family ended up in turmoil and catastrophe."

Tejas inquired, "Daksh, what's troubling you?"

Daksh responded, "I'm Advik; that was my nickname."

Tejas inquired further, "Did you cause harm to your mother?"

Daksh admitted, "Yes, I committed that crime because of my destructive habits."

Daksh said, "It's a sad truth that we often overlook and underestimate our parents' tireless efforts in our favour until the weight of time bears down upon us. This profound realisation seldom dawns upon us until we step into the roles of parents ourselves. It's at that moment of becoming parents that we embark on a poignant journey of rediscovery.

In the depths of parenthood, we unravel the complex tapestry of our own parents' emotions, piecing together their sacrifices and choices. We not only comprehend their actions but also glimpse into the depths of their love and concern, once obscured by our youthful ignorance.

And as this newfound insight blooms within us, it transforms into a profound appreciation, a heartfelt gratitude for the unwavering commitment they showed throughout their lives. Their sacrifices, their selflessness, and their ceaseless devotion all become vividly clear.

With this clarity, an unshakable resolve takes root within us—a pledge to replicate the same level of care, dedication, and love for our children. We realise that the best way to honour our parents' legacy is to pass on the legacy of love and devotion to the generations that follow."

Daksh said, "Throughout the journey of life, we inevitably encounter regrets—some minor, others profound. How we confront these regrets can define the trajectory of our existence. They can serve as the sparks igniting our personal growth, or they can plunge us into a disheartening abyss of self-condemnation and despair."

I find myself burdened with regrets, a catalogue of choices made and unmade, a litany of words spoken in anger, and a profound sorrow for the life I have led. Equally, I am haunted by the life I never lived; the opportunities left untapped, and the failure to evolve into someone other than the person I have become.

But it's not just the weight of personal regrets that bears down upon me; it's also the poignant nostalgia for the love and sacrifices of my mother and father that fills my heart with an indescribable ache. Their unwavering dedication, their sacrifices, and their love etched deeply into my soul are now woven into the fabric of my regrets, reminding me of the paths taken and the moments forever lost.

Tears welled up in Tejas' eyes, and his voice trembled with emotion as he expressed, "Daksh, I hold you in the highest regard because of the journey I've undertaken alongside you. You've transformed my life effortlessly, and I struggle to find the words to convey just how much you mean to me. I can't fathom what my life would have been like if our paths hadn't crossed."

Pursuit of happiness

"Embrace the liberating power of true freedom, found in an unburdened heart that doesn't cling to any object, activity, or circumstance, for therein lies the path to boundless serenity."

– Shree Shambav

Shree Shambav and his group of devotees were taking a break beneath a massive banyan tree when they spotted an older gentleman approaching from a distance. The elderly man appeared fatigued and in search of a place to rest.

Shree Shambav inquired, "Sir, may I know your name?"

The elderly man responded, "I am Manu."

Shree Shambav offered, "Manu, please have some food and water."

After several hours of rest beneath the tree, Manu felt revitalised.

Shree Shambav inquired, "What motivates you to journey under this scorching sun?"

Manu replied, "In the adjacent jungle, there are precious herbs. By gathering a few, I can earn some money to assist my granddaughter."

Shree Shambav inquired, "How old is your granddaughter?"

Manu replied, "She is seven years old."

Shree Shambav simply nodded in response.

Manu then asked, "Shree Shambav, what is the source of desire?"

Shree Shambav remarked, "In the depths of our hearts, we nurture our unique desires. It's like the hunger that stirs within a person, dreaming of a sumptuous meal even when their stomach grumbles in hunger. Or, consider the individual who longs for the sweetness of life, despite the bitter reality of diabetes. And then there's the child, their innocent eyes filled with dreams of cricket matches on the sun-kissed field, an escape from the pages of textbooks. These desires, diverse and powerful, are the very threads that weave the tapestry of our existence, each one telling a story of yearning and hope."

In response, Aditi inquired, "What is the origin of these desires?"

Shree Shambav explained, "Aditi, the root of desire lies in the mind's attachment. When the mind becomes tethered to a particular object or person, it continuously generates desires revolving around that entity. By meditating on the objects of our senses, we form attachments to them, and these attachments inevitably give rise to desires."

Shree Shambav explained, "The influence of passion leads the soul to a delusion, convincing it that worldly possessions hold the key to satisfaction. Consequently, desires are born as we yearn to acquire these possessions."

Within us, the mind functions as a subtle machinery, tirelessly producing thoughts that manifest as desires. Coexisting within the same system is the intellect, the faculty of discrimination. It is the intellect that decides to, while the mind generates desires. Remarkably, the intellect possesses the capacity to govern the mind, even though this might not appear evident at first glance.

Shambav began, "Allow me to recount a poignant allegory. Once, a hunter embarked on his evening stroll along the edge of a forest. Because of the previous day's rain, the path was slippery despite his cautious steps. Despite his efforts, he slipped and tumbled into a small ditch. As he regained his composure and cleaned himself up, he realised that his gun had been lost in the fall. Recognising the risk of being unarmed in the wilderness, he decided it was time to head home.

He began his journey, but as the sun dipped below the horizon, the forest grew dimmer. Determined to find the shortest way out, he made haste, only to discover a group of animals congregating ahead. Before he could devise a plan, these fierce creatures began pursuing him, propelling him deeper into the forest. In his desperate flight, he suddenly encountered a witch, her arms outstretched, as if ready to envelop him.

To evade her grasp, he quickly veered in a new direction, running parallel to both the pursuing animals and the lurking witch."

After a prolonged chase, the forest had become shrouded in darkness. He pressed onward, but eventually, he stumbled and hurtled headfirst, realising that he had fallen off a cliff. At that moment, he was certain that his end was near, yet the pitch-black night offered no clues to his surroundings.

After some time, he perceived his feet were ensnared by a vine, causing him to dangle upside down.

As the hours passed, the first rays of morning sunlight roused him from his stupor. He regained his senses and noticed a snake perched on a large boulder, patiently waiting for him to fall. Simultaneously, he observed two mice, one white and the other black, nibbling at the very branch from which the vine suspended him. To add to his troubles, a swarm of bees gathered, delivering painful stings to his face.

In this precarious predicament, the hunter found an unexpected source of solace, and against all odds, he wore a smile on his face.

A wise observer, who witnessed this extraordinary situation, contemplated how the hunter could maintain a smile in such dire circumstances. He keenly examined the scene and eventually noticed a beehive positioned above the hunter's head, with honey slowly dripping onto his lips. The hunter was savouring the sweetness.

Approaching the hunter, the wise man inquired, "Dear hunter, what is the source of your unwavering smile?"

The hunter responded, "You must taste this honey; it's truly delightful."

The wise man, feeling perplexed, questioned himself, "Can a mere drop of honey bring happiness in the face of such dire circumstances? He is besieged by threats - a perilous fall from the boulder, a menacing snake, the risk of returning to the cliff with the vine, and the looming danger of ferocious animals and a malevolent witch."

Puzzled and unable to find an explanation, the wise man eventually departed from the scene, contemplating whether he might be the one who was losing his mind.

Shree Shambav said, "Indeed, we reside in a world cloaked in illusion, entangled in the relentless web of desire. We often tirelessly pursue goals and objects without truly comprehending the profound truth that underlies our existence. While we may perceive the hunter in this allegorical tale as somewhat bewildered, his journey serves as a poignant reflection of the human condition, one deeply entwined with the beguiling forces of illusion and desire."

Aditi inquired, "Master, could you please enlighten me on the concepts of illusion and desire?"

Shree Shambav began, "The forest through which the hunter traversed symbolises the material world we inhabit, a place fraught with imminent perils at every turn. His gun embodies his true path and purpose. The tumble from the cliff signifies a deviation from that path. The relentless pursuit of ferocious animals mirrors the diseases that gradually manifest in life, persistently plaguing us until our journey's end. And the witch, representing old age, patiently awaits us, ready to embrace us with the passage of time."

"The snake and the boulder at the pit's base serve as metaphors for the inescapable death that ultimately awaits each of us. The white and black mice, nibbling away at the branch, symbolise the ceaseless passage of day and night, steadily diminishing our existence and drawing us nearer to our mortality. The bees, with their stings to the face, represent the countless desires that emerge within our minds, incessantly agitating our inner world and subjecting us to suffering and anguish."

Shree Shambav explained, "The honey serves as a representation of the worldly pleasures that often obscure the clarity of our minds and intellect. Consequently, we become oblivious to our vulnerable state and immerse ourselves in the transient gratifications of our senses. It is the intense, lustful desires that bear responsibility for concealing our power of discrimination."

Shree Shambav continued, "Desire, akin to an insatiable fire, rages endlessly, bestowing no genuine happiness upon anyone. The wise, recognising desire as the wellspring of suffering, relinquish its hold, while those who remain oblivious to this truth fritter away their lives in fruitless endeavours, attempting to quench their insatiable thirst for it."

I think both are the dream

"In the aftermath of this bewildering revelation, amidst the tumultuous waves of confusion, clarity emerges from the depths of the unknown like a beacon of hope, guiding our way forward."

- *Shree Shambav*

During one of Shree Shambav's journeys with his devotees, they encountered a man standing precariously at the edge of a cliff, his gaze fixed intently on the horizon. One of Shree Shambav's disciples, Ashwin, hurriedly approached the man and inquired, "May I know your name, sir?"

In response, the man offered a wry smile and remarked, "In the very next moment, I shall be shattered into pieces, and yet you ask for my name."

Ashwin persisted, saying, "Please, may I have your name?"

After a prolonged moment of contemplation, the man finally replied, "I am Deven."

Ashwin continued, "Deven, it's a fine name. But what has brought you to the precipice like this? Why are you willing to relinquish this invaluable life?"

Deven responded, "You might not comprehend the depths of my experiences, and even if I were to elucidate, I doubt you could offer help."

Ashwin chuckled heartily and replied, "Just a few years ago, I found myself in a situation quite akin to this, utterly distraught and on the brink of breaking. It was then that my own master came to my aid."

Deven was taken aback and inquired, "Who is your master?"

Ashwin gestured towards Shree Shambav, who, along with the other devotees, was taking a rest beneath the tree. Ashwin then approached Deven and formally presented him to Shree Shambav.

"I have a lot of problems and bad memories, and I'm not able to come out of it," Deven cried. The only way I can get out of it is to commit suicide."

Shree Shambav inquired, “May I comprehend the challenges you’ve faced?”

Deven recounted, “In my youth, I experienced the loss of both my parents. After persevering through many hardships, I embarked on my entrepreneurial journey, and my business initially thrived. I managed to acquire my land and home. A few years later, I entered into a marriage with a kind and supportive partner, and we were blessed with two children. Everything was sailing smoothly until one unfortunate day when a devastating fire swept through, causing me to lose all my possessions and plunge into debt. Consequently, my demeanour towards my family soured, and my once-happy family life took a bitter turn. Nonetheless, my wife displayed remarkable kindness and made earnest efforts to help me regain my composure. Gradually, my business began to recover, and life returned to a semblance of normalcy.”

With a heavy heart, Deven continued his sombre tale, his voice quivering with the weight of sorrow. "One fateful day, I embarked on a journey to the town to purchase some much-needed goods. Little did I know that nature had cruel plans in store. The sky wept incessantly, and the heavens unleashed a torrential downpour. The rain swelled the once-tranquil river into a monstrous, raging beast, and in its merciless embrace, it claimed the lives of all the villagers."

Tears welled up in Deven's eyes as he recalled the heart-wrenching moment. "When I finally returned home, the world as I knew it had been mercilessly washed away. My house was but a memory, and the walls that once echoed with the laughter of my beloved wife and children now stood swallowed by the relentless floodwaters. I searched tirelessly, calling out their names into the unforgiving darkness, but my cries were met only with the haunting silence of despair."

His voice quivered, breaking under the unbearable weight of uncertainty. "Since that dreadful day, I have scoured every corner of this world, clinging to a flicker of hope that they might still exist, that they might have survived the wrath of nature. But the cruel hands of fate have kept their fate hidden from me. I am adrift in a sea of emptiness, with no one left to hold on to, and I find myself questioning the very purpose of my existence."

Deven's gaze pleaded with his listener, seeking an answer to the most profound question that tormented his soul. "Does my presence in this world hold any significance? Can it make a difference, a single ray of light in the darkness that has enveloped my life?"

Shree Shambav sat in attentive silence, his eyes gently closed, while Deven poured out his heart. After several moments of quiet contemplation, Shree Shambav broke the silence with empathetic words. "Deven, each one of us navigates life through diverse circumstances, laden with sufferings, pains, and formidable challenges. At times, the fog of confusion descends upon us, and we begin to question whether the burdens we carry are indeed our own."

Observing Deven's tearful state, Shree Shambav urged him to reflect more deeply on the profound struggles he endured. "Take a moment to ponder, Deven, the anguish you've endured, the agony that courses through your veins, and the tribulations that surround you. Ask yourself whether they are worthy adversaries of the precious gift of life you possess."

Shree Shambav said, "Allow me to share a tale of a prince named Siddharth, who grappled with a mysterious ailment, the final throes of life tightening their grip on him. Siddharth was the sole heir to the throne, his father being the esteemed King Aditya. Despite exhausting every conceivable remedy and summoning the most skilled physicians from every corner of his vast kingdom, Siddharth's health continued to deteriorate, and no medicine could offer him respite. After an exhaustive pursuit of a cure, it became painfully apparent that all that remained was to await the inevitable."

One of the physicians in the king's service spoke with a heavy heart, addressing the monarch, "Your Majesty, despite our unwavering efforts, we can only hope that his passing may come without prolonged suffering."

Upon hearing these words, the queen's tears flowed freely, and an air of profound emotion enveloped everyone in the presence of the anguished king.

The king inquired, "Physician, can you tell me how much time he has left?"

The physician initially hesitated, taking a moment before responding, "Your Majesty, he will not survive until sunrise; this night will be his last."

Upon hearing these words, the king was overcome with sorrow, yet he also consoled himself with the inevitability of death. Recognising the certainty of the situation, the king took a seat beside his ailing son, determined to stay awake throughout the entire night, keeping vigil by his side.

The king cherished the precious memories he had shared with his son, struggling to come to terms with the impending loss of his only child in the coming years. A whirlwind of thoughts and emotions swirled in his mind as the early hours of dawn drew nearer. Eventually, the weariness overcame him, and despite his inner turmoil, the king succumbed to sleep. In slumber, his worries and concerns dissolved, granting him a peaceful respite.

In the depths of slumber, the king was granted a wondrous dream. In this dream, he reigned as a powerful monarch, the ruler of the entire universe. His heart swelled with joy as he gazed upon his beautiful and healthy children, each radiating intelligence and beauty. Beside him stood his beloved, the epitome of kindness and grace. Their abode was a magnificent golden palace, adorned with unimaginable wealth and precious jewels, symbols of his boundless prosperity.

His name echoed far and wide as he commanded the mightiest of armies and was beloved by every soul within his realm. On this day, a grand celebration engulfed the kingdom, and the air resonated with the joyous cheers of his subjects. The king and his family revelled in the festivities with unbridled exuberance.

Yet, amid his blissful reverie, as he dwelt deeply in the dream's embrace, his only son drew his final breath in the waking world. The piercing cry of the queen, echoing with profound loss and agony, shattered the tranquillity of the dream. The anguished wail reverberated in his slumbering ears, accompanied by the frantic footsteps of those who rushed to the scene.

The cacophony of grief and despair yanked the king from his idyllic reverie, tearing him away from the empire he had momentarily possessed. His golden palace vanished into thin air, and his beautiful children dissolved like mirages. The gentle, kind queen faded from his sight, and his abundance of treasure disappeared into the void. In an instant, the king's world crumbled before him, and he awoke to a reality where his son had departed, his queen mourned in agony, and his entire kingdom wept for the loss of their future ruler.

Amidst these tumultuous events, the king bore a serene countenance, his lips adorned with a gentle smile. Observing this peculiar display, the queen couldn't contain her bewilderment. She inquired, "What has come over you? Have you, my lord, turned impervious to sorrow? Is it possible that you don't grieve for the loss of our son? You appear so different now, even though our child has departed, you wear a smile."

In response, Aditya, with a contemplative look, said, "I find myself in a bewildering quandary, my love. Should my heart be heavy with grief for the son who now rests in eternal slumber, or should it swell with joy for the fleeting glimpse I had of our beautiful children just moments ago? Should I mourn the loss of an empire that stretched across the universe, an abundance of wealth, and the opulent splendour of a golden palace? Or should I celebrate the memory of a life where I commanded the mightiest of armies? In the blink of an eye, all I possessed dissolved into the void as soon as I opened my eyes."

Aditya's voice trembled with a deep well of emotion as he spoke, his words laden with profound reflection. "As I closed my eyes, the image of my son in his final moments did not even cross my mind. Instead, I revelled in the joy of playing with my vibrant, healthy children. It was a moment of bliss. But the instant I beheld my son on his deathbed, the fleeting joy I had experienced vanished like a wisp of smoke. At that moment, it felt as though I had lost not only my son but also all the beautiful children I had cherished in the sanctuary of my closed eyes."

With a heavy heart and a furrowed brow, Aditya's voice held a note of anguish as he grappled with the profound dilemma before him. "Which of these experiences is the truth? I find myself ensnared in a web of confusion, uncertain of how to reconcile these conflicting emotions. What path should I tread now, in the wake of this bewildering revelation?"

Aditya's words carried a profound weight of emotion as he pressed on, grappling with the agonising choices before him. "Should my tears fall for the child who now lies before me, or should they flow for the children I lost the moment I opened my eyes? In that sacred realm behind closed lids, I basked in happiness and revelled in a state of pure bliss. Yet, as soon as I dared to open my eyes, I was confronted with a world marred by suffering and agony. Two dreams, both vivid and yet worlds apart, unfolded within the realms of my consciousness. It dawns upon me that they are but dreams – one, a dream of unadulterated bliss, and the other, a haunting vision of suffering and pain."

Shree Shambav gently spoke to Deven, encouraging him to introspect. "Deven, let us begin to question the trauma we endure, the pain we feel, the emotions that grip us, and the suffering we endure. Do they truly have an independent existence, or are they merely the constructs of our beliefs, illusions woven by our thoughts that convince us of their reality?"

Shree Shambav added, "Deven, could it be that our beliefs and illusions, in their entirety, stem from our attachments? The deeper our attachments, the more profound the pain we must endure. Perhaps it is the intensity of our connections that ultimately shapes the illusions we grapple with."

A Beautiful Flower

"In the depths of sincere exploration, we discover the soul-stirring beauty hidden beneath the surface, a beauty more profound and pure than what the eye can behold. It is in the ardent pursuit of understanding that we unveil life's authentic treasures, and in doing so, we unearth the very essence of existence."

- *Shree Shambav*

One day, as Shree Shambav and his devoted followers embarked on a journey through various villages, they encountered diverse individuals along the way. Their first encounter was with a man who appeared impoverished, clad in tattered clothing. One follower commented on his appearance, remarking on his humble attire.

Continuing their travels, they came upon another soul afflicted by a severe skin ailment, which caused blood and pus to seep from his wounds. Another follower commented on the unpleasant odour emanating from the man's injuries.

Further along the path, they encountered a man with a physical disability, his hair unkempt and appearance weathered. One follower expressed unease at the sight of him, finding his appearance unsettling.

Throughout these encounters, Shree Shambav remained silent, listening to the conversations of his devotees. Undeterred by the varying appearances of those they met, he pressed on with his journey.

After an extensive journey, they sought respite and discovered a majestic tree surrounded by lush greenery, with a serene stream nearby. Shree Shambav and his devoted followers refreshed themselves with crystal-clear waters and savoured the goodness of fresh fruits.

Following their arduous and exhausting journey, the weary travellers decided to pause, seeking solace in much-needed rest. After dedicating several hours to rejuvenating their tired bodies and spirits, they gathered around Shree Shambav, who, with a depth of wisdom in his eyes, initiated his discourse.

"In the vast tapestry of life," he began, his voice resonating with profound insight, "there exists a timeless adage - 'All that glitters is not gold.' This adage carries a poignant message that extends far beyond its words. It serves as a reminder that appearances can be deceiving and that not everything that shimmers with the allure of value truly possesses it. This truth applies to the myriad facets of our existence, be it individuals, places, or objects, all of which may assert their worthiness, yet often conceal a shallowness beneath their surface.

"In our journey through life," Shree Shambav continued, "we must refrain from forming hasty judgments based solely on outward appearances. Instead, we must embark on a quest to uncover their genuine essence, their intrinsic worth, for it is only by delving deeper into the heart of things that we can discern their true value. Let us not be swayed by the glimmering facade, but let us seek the authenticity that lies beneath."

Shree Shambav proceeded, "Allow me to share a tale from ages past. In those distant days, a venerable saint by the name of Jaya set forth a task for his devoted followers. He entrusted this disciple with the quest to retrieve the most exquisite and exceedingly rare flower that could be found in the nearby forest. With meticulous detail, he provided a vivid description of the flower's appearance."

Guided by their comprehension of the saint's instructions, the devoted followers embarked on their quest. However, despite an entire day spent in fervent search, the elusive flower remained beyond their grasp. As the sun began its descent, casting the landscape in shadows and deepening the encroaching darkness, a sense of concern began to pervade the group. Some among them voiced their unease, suggesting, "Perhaps it is time for us to return."

Adi explained, "Under our master's guidance, we have not yet obtained the desired flower. Therefore, returning at this juncture would not be appropriate."

Ultimately, they resolved to remain in the forest, determined to acquire the elusive flower without further hindrance. The night was spent amidst the forest's embrace, and with the dawn of a new day, they resumed their journey.

The following day, they devised a plan to venture into the dense, shadowy forest. As they delved deeper into the heart of the woods, exhaustion, hunger, and thirst began to take their toll. Despite their diligent efforts to locate water sources that might relieve their parched throats, their search proved futile. Even after an extended quest, the precious liquid remained elusive, and the mounting worry gave rise to a sense of uncertainty and fear that gradually seeped into their hearts.

A concerned devotee spoke up, expressing their dire predicament, "Should we fail to locate water to satisfy our thirst, our fate may be sealed, and one by one, we could succumb."

As the hours passed and the relentless thirst and dehydration took their toll, the devotees began to weaken, succumbing to faintness one by one. Among them, Adi found himself at a loss, grappling with the gravity of the situation and searching for a way to address it.

In his desperate search for aid, Adi spotted a figure in the distance, and with a glimmer of hope, he ventured toward the stranger, extending an earnest plea for assistance.

Adi inquired, "Sir, could you kindly direct me to a source of water to alleviate our thirst?"

The man, who was a hunter, responded with curiosity, “Adi, what circumstances have brought you to this remote location?”

The hunter cautioned, “This area is perilously infested with venomous insects and reptiles.”

Adi explained, “Our purpose here is to adhere to our master’s guidance, seeking the most exquisite and exceptionally rare flower.”

Without delay, both Adi and the hunter hurried toward the nearby stream. They collected water and used it to revive the ailing devotees, helping them reach the stream. Gratefully, all the devotees quenched their thirst and extended their heartfelt appreciation to the hunter for his assistance.

Adi, accompanied by the hunter, swiftly approached the unconscious devotees, and administered water to revive them, ensuring their well-being.

The hunter cautioned, “To discover that exquisite flower, you must venture deeper into the forest. However, be forewarned, the path ahead is treacherous and fraught with peril.”

Expressing their gratitude, Adi and his fellow devotees conveyed their appreciation to the hunter before resuming their journey.

With a description of the route, they needed to follow, the hunter took his leave, allowing them to proceed on their quest.

As the devotees pressed on with their journey, the terrain grew increasingly rugged, and the presence of untamed wildlife became more apparent. The sight of these wild creatures struck fear into the hearts of some of the devotees, who feared imminent harm or even death at the hands of these animals. Shivers of anxiety coursed through their bodies, yet driven by their unwavering commitment to fulfilling their mission, they soldiered on.

However, their determination was soon interrupted by a piercing scream of agony from one of their own. Adi and the fellow devotees hurried to the source of the distress, discovering that their companion had fallen victim to a snakebite. They glimpsed the venomous serpent slithering away into the underbrush, leaving the suffering devotee writhing in pain. In the face of this dire situation, they found themselves at a loss, uncertain of how to provide aid. The gravity of the situation weighed heavily upon them, as they understood that without swift intervention, their fellow devotee's life hung in the balance.

From a distance, Adi spotted a modest hut and hurriedly guided his companions toward it. A man, clad in worn and soiled attire, emerged from the humble dwelling and inquired, "How may I be of assistance?"

Tears welled up in the eyes of all the devotees, their worry palpable as they explained, "Our friend is in dire straits, and if he doesn't receive aid promptly, his life hangs in the balance."

The man attentively examined the snakebite and reassured the anxious devotees, saying, "Dear devotees, there is no need for undue concern."

Using a small, finely honed blade, the man delicately incised the wound and drew out the venom with his mouth. After a brief respite, the afflicted devotee was offered a soothing cup of herbal tea, gradually restoring him to his normal state. A collective sense of relief and gratitude washed over all the devotees, and they warmly expressed their thanks to the man for his lifesaving intervention.

Curious about the man's extraordinary ability, Adi inquired, "Sir, may I ask how you possessed the knowledge and skill to aid our friend?"

The man offered insight into his remarkable expertise, explaining, "My family and I have inhabited this forest for generations, and we have developed a deep understanding of the flora and fauna here. We have honed our knowledge of treating snakebites using the herbs readily available to us."

The humble wife of the impoverished man kindly extended an invitation, saying, "I urge all the devotees to remain with us for the night, as you appear quite fatigued."

Adi and the other devoted travellers readily accepted the gracious offer to stay and find rest. The couple generously provided them with a nourishing meal and arranged a comfortable place for them to rest. Adi and his fellow devotees were deeply moved by the warmth and assistance they had received during their stay. As dawn approached, it was time for them to bid farewell and continue their journey.

The man cautioned, "Adi, the path ahead is marked by steep, rugged terrain, and treacherous slippery slopes. You must exercise utmost caution and pay meticulous attention to every step."

With heartfelt gratitude, Adi and his fellow devotees expressed they're thanks to the impoverished man and his family for their kindness and assistance. They then departed, resolute in their mission to complete the journey ahead.

Adi cautioned, "Our journey demands great care, for any misstep could cause dire consequences, potentially costing us our lives. Therefore, each one of us must proceed with meticulous slowness and utmost caution." As they approached the cliff's edge, nearly all of them had successfully reached this critical point. However, their collective anticipation was met with disappointment as they scoured the area, failing to locate the elusive, rare flower.

Exhausted and disheartened, Adi and his fellow devotees lamented, "Despite our unwavering dedication and the considerable risks we've undertaken to reach this pinnacle, our endeavours have yielded no fruit."

After several hours filled with a profound sense of disappointment and sadness, their attention was drawn to a peculiar figure passing by in the distance. One of the devotees remarked, "Observe that man's appearance; it sends shivers down my spine."

Overcoming their initial reservations, one of the devoted individuals cautiously approached the stranger and inquired, "Could you kindly direct us to the location of the exceedingly rare and beautiful flower?"

A warm smile graced the man's face as he responded, "Please, join me."

Though the devotees had harboured some initial concerns, they found themselves with no other option but to accompany the man on his quest to find the elusive flower. Reluctantly, they followed him, and their journey ultimately led them to the banks of a serene stream. There, their eyes were greeted by the breathtaking sight of the coveted flower, and a wave of excitement and joy washed over them, erasing all the pain and hardship they had endured in an instant.

Adi inquired, "Sir, may we be permitted to gather a few of these flowers for ourselves?"

The man, observing the weariness etched on their faces, responded compassionately, "You all appear quite exhausted. I suggest you take a well-deserved rest for a few days, and then you can collect these flowers."

Adi and the fellow devotees readily accepted the man's thoughtful advice. They chose to stay at his abode for two days, during which they immersed themselves in the serene embrace of nature, revelling in its true beauty.

Upon their departure, Adi and his companions extended their heartfelt gratitude to the man for his benevolence and warm hospitality. They left his home, their hearts uplifted, and the precious flower in tow.

The man advised, "You can bypass the lengthy path you've already traversed and instead follow a shorter, less perilous route to return to your abode." He described an alternative path that was not only shorter but considerably less hazardous, leading them safely back to their home.

Ultimately, they arrived back home, the rare flower still radiantly fresh in their possession. Upon their return, they presented the precious bloom to their master, Jaya. To their surprise, he instructed them to place it in a corner, a response that left Adi and the rest of the devoted followers utterly bewildered. Their master's lack of enthusiasm for the beautiful flower was unexpected and puzzling.

After several days, Jaya inquired of his devoted followers, "Does this flower still keep its brilliance?"

Adi replied, "Master, while it was indeed magnificent when it was freshly plucked, it has since faded in its charm and brilliance."

Curious about their journey, Jaya inquired, "Tell me, was your expedition filled with excitement?" Adi and the other devotees proceeded to vividly recount the details of their lengthy and thrilling journey, with Jaya attentively and silently listening.

Following the recitation of their narrative, Jaya fell into a contemplative silence, allowing a few minutes to pass. Then, he posed a reflective question, asking, "For how long do you believe this flower will linger in your memories?"

Adi and his fellow devotees responded, "We anticipate that the memory of this flower will linger in our minds for the next few months."

Jaya then inquired, "And what do you believe will be the most enduring memory from your journey?" One of the devotees promptly replied, "It would undoubtedly be the recollection of the man who rescued me from the brink of death by providing the means to quench my insatiable thirst. Without his timely help, my life may have been lost."

The second devotee shared, "My lasting memory would be of the man who rescued me from a venomous snakebite. He was my guardian angel."

The third devotee added, "For me, it will be the memory of the man who acted as our guide, leading us to the flowers when we were lost and clueless."

Jaya, with a knowing smile, remarked, "It seems that the memory of this beautiful flower will pale in comparison to the indelible impressions left by the compassionate souls you encountered on your journey."

Shree Shambav said, "Much like this exquisite flower, appearances often serve as veils that obscure the true essence beneath. Many things may dazzle with their superficial charm, yet upon closer examination or lived experience, they often reveal themselves as empty and futile. It is a profound truth that one cannot gauge the worth of a person, place, or thing merely by their external facade. In the course of your journey, you encountered the hunter, the impoverished man, and the unassuming stranger, and in them, you discovered a deeper truth—a beauty, purity, and preciousness that transcended the surface.

"Every glittering stone is not necessarily precious, and not every shining metal is gold. To truly discern the value and nature of things, we must be willing to delve deeper, to invest the effort in understanding the beauty that lies beneath. It is through this pursuit that we uncover the genuine treasures in life, far more precious and purer than what meets the eye."

Human nature has long been susceptible to the allure of what is good and beautiful. Yet, it remains a universal truth that many individuals, regardless of appearances, succumb to the seduction of external beauty. It is only the wise who draw invaluable lessons from their experiences, for they understand that one's character cannot be discerned from a smiling countenance, a cheerful demeanour, or a well-mannered facade.

Time and again, history has shown that individuals have concealed their true selves in their relentless pursuit of personal gain. Behind the veneer of high moral standards and virtuous displays lies an inner reality of shallowness and vanity. This practice of masking one's true nature with a dazzling facade is a means to deceive and mislead others.

Shree Shambav said, “It is deceptively easy to manipulate and misguide people by assuming the guise of goodness, donning fine garments, and delivering eloquent speeches. The human mind, often gullible and naïve, is readily swayed by the polite manners and attractive appearances of such individuals. It is a crucial lesson that one should internalise from an early age. Being discerning, logical, and reasonable before rushing to conclusions is paramount. Embracing a life of simplicity, coupled with thoughtful and righteous thinking, paves the way for a virtuous existence.”

A wise man and a stone

"Empty your mind of all thoughts. Let your heart be at peace. In the silence of your soul, you shall discover the profound depths of serenity."

- *Shree Shambav*

A wandering elderly sage named Darpan was joyfully journeying through the mountains when he encountered a dog. While the dog introduced itself as Amar. Together, they made the most of what nature offered during their travels, seeking the finest resting spots along their path. Darpan led a contented and harmonious life in this manner.

On a particular day during their journey, they stumbled upon a remarkable discovery—a precious stone nestled in a crystal-clear stream. This gem was sizeable and held the promise of substantial wealth, offering Darpan security for a lifetime. With great care, Darpan picked up the precious stone, ensuring that no prying eyes were upon him, and gently placed it inside his bag.

As they continued their journey, a whirlwind of thoughts swirled in Darpan's mind. The precious stone he had discovered held the potential to transform his life, but gradually, his joy gave way to anxiety. He sensed a looming presence, a feeling that someone might tail him, driven by a desire to possess his newfound gem. This mounting fear compelled Darpan and his faithful companion, Amar, to hasten their pace until exhaustion overtook them.

Now, Darpan grappled with the pressing concern of safeguarding the precious stone. It became evident to him that keeping it within his bag was far from secure.

He was consumed by thoughts of finding the optimal hiding place for the stone.

As days passed, Darpan's unease grew. His appetite dwindled, and sleep eluded him, leaving him weak and frail. His once-vibrant enthusiasm waned, and he lost interest in everything around him, even his loyal companion, Amar.

Amar remained silent, quietly observing the unfolding events.

For Darpan, all other interests and ambitions faded into insignificance. His sole purpose and aspiration revolved around attaining wealth by selling the precious stone to a merchant residing in the nearby town. As they drew closer to the town, Darpan eagerly reached into his bag to retrieve the precious gem, only to find it missing.

In an instant, Darpan's dreams of a prosperous and luxurious life were shattered. He erupted in anguished cries, utterly bewildered by how he could have lost the precious stone. He had been vigilant throughout the journey, and in the very moment when his long-cherished desire seemed within reach, it had all crumbled away.

Darpan felt lost, uncertain about his future and what steps to take next. He grappled with confusion, wondering how he could carry on with life.

In a moment of despair, Darpan muttered to himself, "There seems to be no purpose in continuing; maybe I should put an end to it." Fuelled by anger and disappointment, he hurried towards the nearby cliff, seemingly on the verge of taking a drastic step.

Witnessing this, Amar, with tears welling up in his eyes, rushed forward and prevented Darpan from proceeding further.

Amar questioned, "What have I done wrong to make you want to abandon me?"

Amar continued, "I have remained loyal and devoted to you, and we shared happiness long before we discovered the stone. However, everything changed after finding it."

Amar pressed on, "Does that gleaming stone hold greater worth than my presence in your life or even your own life?"

Amar's inquiry struck Darpan like a bolt of lightning, abruptly awakening him to the realisation that something had taken a dark turn. He gathered his thoughts and sought to comfort himself, and together, they descended from the cliff. Eventually, they settled beside a serene lake, where they sat in silence for hours on end.

As Darpan gazed upon his reflection in the tranquil lake, he embarked on a profound introspection. He began to question himself with a heavy heart, "Why am I so distraught? Why have I become so entangled with that stone? Does the key to my happiness truly lie within that gem? Is it my insatiable greed that has led me down this path, robbing me of peaceful nights and drowning me in anger and frustration?"

In his contemplation, Darpan continued, "Once, I was fearless and enjoyed a sound, peaceful sleep. We revelled in the simple joys of our journey, and now I see that I have relinquished my true precious gem—the true beauty of life itself—by obsessing over a small, lifeless stone."

After observing in silence for an extended period, Amar finally spoke, his words tinged with profound wisdom and emotion. He addressed his master, saying, "My dear master, it is the senses, the mind, and the intellect that often give birth to desires. These desires have cast a shadow over your understanding, leading your pure soul astray. During this journey, you lose sight of yourself. You sacrificed your happiness, neglected your basic needs such as hunger and sleep, and became consumed by restlessness and anger. You even overlooked my hunger. If you persist in living a life filled with confusion and doubt, you will find only misery, devoid of happiness, both within and in the external world."

Darpan, struck by the truth in Amar's words, felt a deep sense of remorse for his past behaviour. Together, they resumed their journey. Along the way, they revisited the same stream and stumbled upon another precious stone resting on its banks.

Amar remarked, "Master, look at that valuable gem; it's even larger than the previous one."

This time, Darpan's reaction was more subdued. He simply retrieved the stone and placed it in his bag, and they continued their journey.

Amar added, "Master, you can shape your life anew with this gem."

Darpan grinned and replied, "Amar, it's merely a stone. Desire and greed had once clouded my judgment and misled my soul. I'm unwilling to forfeit my happiness for the sake of this gleaming piece of stone."

As they continued their journey, they encountered a famished traveller. Darpan opened his bag to share some food, and in doing so, the hungry traveller caught sight of the precious stone. He requested the elderly man to give it to him.

Without a moment's hesitation, Darpan handed over the stone. The traveller departed, his heart filled with gratitude for his newfound fortune, fully aware that this stone held the promise of security for a lifetime.

Darpan and Amar resumed their journey with a sense of contentment. However, several days later, the same traveller hurriedly returned to deliver the gem to the wise old man.

The traveller spoke with earnestness, saying, “I’ve pondered deeply on this matter. I recognise the immense worth of the stone, yet I return it to you, harbouring a different hope. I seek that which resides within you, something far more precious than any gem. I yearn for the inner wisdom and generosity that enabled you to part with the stone so freely.”

Darpan’s smile deepened, and he gazed at Amar for a timeless moment before sharing his wisdom through a profound anecdote:

“Imagine,” he began, “Your mind is like a vast field, teeming with thoughts that flutter like restless birds. In this grand field, let us cultivate tranquillity, where the heart can find its true serenity.”

With a tone brimming with emotion, Darpan continued, “Embrace contentment with what you possess today. Release the burden of longing for what you lack, and in this, you shall discover true happiness. What you possess today may slip through your fingers tomorrow, just as the morning dew evaporates with the rising sun. Yet, what you yearn for, what remains a distant dream, may one day find its way to your doorstep. So, live your life as it is."

Darpan concluded, "Live as you are, for in that simplicity, you shall find the richest tapestry of all."

King and A Monk

"Belief resides in the mind, while faith inhabits the very essence of your being. Belief can be borrowed, but faith is born from the crucible of your personal experience, bearing the weight of your soul's journey."

- *Shree Shambav*

Vidhaatri inquired, "Master, I often confuse the terms 'faith' and 'belief.' What distinguishes one from the other?"

The Master responded, "Belief involves recognising something as true or real, especially when there is no substantiating evidence. When you hold a belief, you accept it as true, even in the absence of compelling evidence. Your reasons for firmly embracing a particular idea or statement may lack validity or even be mistaken. It represents a hypothesis or perspective that lacks support from any evidence."

Each belief inherently carries a degree of uncertainty. As you persist in holding onto your beliefs, you do so to suppress doubt, yet it steadily seeps further into your subconscious.

Believing in something or someone necessitates faith, particularly in the absence of clear evidence, even when there's no prior proof of your capability or actions. Faith can serve as the driving force behind your willingness to take risks. Whether it pertains to self-confidence, love, commitment to a partner, or finding happiness in one's environment, it plays a significant role.

The Master said, "Faith represents an enduring belief or confidence in someone or something. Life is filled with unexpected twists and turns, and predicting what will transpire in the next moment is beyond our grasp.

Nevertheless, we persist in our journey through life. Faith serves as a perpetual inner beacon, reinforcing our optimistic outlook on life and motivating us to persevere, regardless of the challenges we encounter."

The Master said, "Allow me to narrate a tale: Each night, King Prithvi would conceal his identity and traverse his capital to ascertain whether everything was in order or if any concealed issues persisted."

One individual, a remarkably alluring and profoundly tranquil man, consistently sat beneath a tree, baffling the king. This man remained there, unwavering and motionless, regardless of the hour of the night when the king made his rounds. Naturally, curiosity began to stir within the king, and eventually, he succumbed to the temptation to learn the man's name and the purpose of his vigil. The man had relinquished all possessions, and the king sought to inquire about his purpose.

"I am Abhaya, and I am safeguarding myself; I have no other duty," the monk responded with a serene smile. "Rather than protecting possessions, I am safeguarding the most profound treasure through complete alertness, mindfulness, and awakening."

Monk persisted, "You possess a multitude of tasks, concerns, and things to safeguard, yet a guardian is conspicuously absent."

The king, perplexed yet deeply fascinated by the man's beauty and the compelling wisdom of his words, engaged in brief conversations with him each night. Over time, a profound friendship developed between them.

Interestingly, the monk never posed the question, "Who are you?"

"I've been posing many inquiries to you over these past days, yet you've never inquired about my identity," the king mentioned.

"If you truly knew the depths of your being," the monk mused, a gentle smile gracing his lips, "you wouldn't find the need to seek answers to these myriad questions. I embrace you exactly as you are, harbouring no intention of causing you any discomfort. Just as I've never inquired about the rising sun, the moon, the stars, the enchanting night sky, the steadfast trees, the flowing river, the myriad animals, or the melodious birds, I see no reason to probe you. In your presence, and that of others, I am at peace, completely at ease."

The monk continued, his voice carrying a profound sense of wisdom and compassion, "The urge to question and know another person often arises from curiosity rooted in unease, tension, and doubt, sometimes even fear. Such curiosity may stem from suspicion, where one might perceive the other as a potential adversary. Yet, it's important to recognise that predictability often accompanies such inquiries."

The monk replied with a profound depth of emotion, "The future remains elusive; every attempt to foretell it carries the potential to elicit joy, anxiety, or sorrow. I find perfect serenity in the embrace of the unknown. Regardless of the unfolding events around me, I remain in a state of tranquil contentment. Life's mysteries only deepen its enchantment. Each passing moment is a breathtaking tapestry of wonder and fragrance, leaving me with no desire for more. It matters not who you are; in your presence, I find solace and deep affection. I hold love for everyone and everything that surrounds me. To put it simply, I love it. I am unaware of any other way to engage with the world."

With unwavering conviction, the monk continued, "In my belief, there is no alternative path to connect with the universe than through love, compassion, and kindness. I expect complete acceptance of the supreme."

The king stood in awe of the monk's profound knowledge and wisdom. Here was an authentic monk who had relinquished all, even clothing, and embraced his surroundings without reservation.

King Prithvi exclaimed with heartfelt admiration, "I have discovered a true and remarkable friend. Your purpose and deep insights inspire me greatly. I eagerly expect the nightfall to converse with you, yet a lingering fear haunts me — the day when you might not be here, having departed."

Turning to the monk, the king inquired, "Abhaya, would you do me the honour of joining me in my palace?"

Undoubtedly, the monk replied, "This is a commendable proposal."

The swift approval from the saint caught the king off guard. He couldn't fathom how the saint, having renounced the world, could entertain the notion of returning to it. A multitude of questions weighed on the king's mind as he contemplated.

"This is indeed an excellent idea," the monk responded. "I can accompany you without delay, for I possess nothing to gather or preparations to arrange."

The king's thoughts became shrouded in uncertainty. He began to question whether he had been deceived. Doubts crept in, suggesting that this man might not be a genuine saint but someone who had been pretending, biding his time for an opportunity like this. Regrettably, it was now too late to rescind the invitation.

With a heavy heart, the king reluctantly agreed to his decision, feeling a sense of regret for what he perceived as a misguided choice.

Returning to his kingdom with someone he had yearned for, loved, and held dear, the king found himself overcome with sadness and hesitation. Upon their arrival, he bestowed upon the monk the finest accommodations, attire, and sustenance.

The king had hoped that the monk would decline the various material comforts offered, including the luxurious bed and the splendid room. However, to the king's surprise, the monk embraced all the luxuries and expressed gratitude to the king for his generosity.

The presence of the monk troubled the king deeply, causing him to toss and turn throughout the night. Worries gnawed at him, questioning whether he had made an error in inviting the monk into the palace, whether the monk was truly genuine, or if he had been deceived. These concerns kept him awake all night, in stark contrast to the monk, who slept peacefully and revelled in the comforts provided.

Over time, the king's trust and admiration for the monk began to erode. He found it increasingly perplexing how the monk indulged in delicious meals, adorned himself in expensive garments, and engaged in conversations with attractive women as if nothing was amiss. The monk's behaviour was consistent with his earlier presence beneath the tree.

King Prithivi's patience had worn thin, his initial disappointment had transformed into seething anger, and he had come to a firm conviction that the monk had exploited him. His desire to expel the monk from his palace had intensified more than ever before.

King Prithivi addressed Abhaya, saying, "Abhaya, there's been a question weighing on my mind for quite some time, yet I've hesitated to ask you. Would it be acceptable for me to inquire, with all due respect?"

The man responded with a smile, "Not merely for a few days, but from the very first moment when I accepted your invitation."

The king found himself in a state of disbelief. "What do you mean?" he inquired.

The monk spoke with profound depth and emotion, and said, "Prithvi, I could see it in your expression, in the depths of your eyes, from the very moment I accepted your invitation. You would have held respect for me if I had declined your offer. However, you must comprehend this - I am a soul that rejects nothing. My acceptance knows no conditions. Your invitation is entirely acceptable. When I remarked that the palace was good, I intended to convey that I am inherently good, irrespective of my surroundings. I was good while sitting naked beneath that tree, just as I am well now, clad in royal robes, amidst the company of beautiful women and surrounded by luxury. I understand your bewilderment; it's evident that you are weary, disheartened, and not your usual self. You may pose your question; even though I already hold the answer, feel free to ask."

The king inquired, "If you are already aware of the question, then the inquiry now becomes: what sets you apart from me?"

The monk responded with a soft chuckle, "Time will unveil the answer to your question. I shall respond when and where it deems fitting."

The monk then proposed, "King, let us embark on an early journey tomorrow morning."

The king, unable to find sleep, impatiently awaited the break of dawn.

As they embarked on their journey the following day, riding on separate horses, the monk revelled in the ride and took the opportunity to share the marvels of nature with the monarch. However, the king remained resistant to embracing the beauty around him and was unwilling to find enjoyment in the experience. Throughout the journey, the king remained silent.

Finally, the king issued a command, saying, "Halt! At this very moment, this river marks the border of my kingdom. I cannot venture beyond this river, for it is the territory of a neighbouring king who has been my adversary for many years. We have already travelled quite a distance, and I have given you ample time to respond to my inquiry. My patience is now exhausted, and I regret extending the invitation into my realm."

With a warm smile, the monk expressed, "I'm grateful for your acceptance into your palace, into your heart. The moment has arrived to shed your robes and return your horse."

He gracefully dismounted the horse and gently removed his robe.

"Thank you, King," the monk continued, "I shall proceed to the other side of the river, for I bear no adversaries. Neither the robe nor this horse was ever truly mine; I possess nothing of my own."

Turning to the king, he asked with sincerity, "Are you prepared to accompany me, or do you choose otherwise?"

The king, his voice laced with astonishment, responded, "How could I possibly join you? My duty lies in safeguarding the kingdom, my family, and my people. Everything I have strived for, struggled for, and aspired to achieve throughout my life is tied to this realm. How could I leave it behind and accompany you?"

The monk responded with a serene smile and said, "That is the distinction between us. I can soar to any destination, unburdened, unchained, and unrestricted, for I carry no possessions, harbour no regrets, bear no baggage, and possess nothing to lose. I treasured each moment as it came, savouring its unique essence. Now, I am destined to cherish the untamed wilderness, the whispering trees, the flowing river, the shimmering stars, the radiant moon, and the warm embrace of the sun."

It was as though King Prithvi had awoken from a haunting nightmare. He grappled with the enormity of his mistake, finding it difficult to come to terms with the repercussions of his actions. The realisation dawned upon him that this man had not deceived him; he was indeed an authentic sage of enlightenment.

"Monk," King Prithvi implored, "I beg your forgiveness. Please do not depart, for I fear I will never forgive myself if you leave."

"I have no objections to returning," the monk replied, "but in the future, you might find reasons to doubt me again. Therefore, it might be wiser to release me now. I'll be waiting on the opposite bank, beneath that beautiful tree. You can visit whenever you like, at least to the other side, and meet me there. I choose not to return, as I wish not to disrupt your peace or burden you with anxiety."

The king's resistance only deepened his feelings of remorse and sorrow, burdened by the guilt of his actions.

"Don't be disheartened," the monk comforted with a gentle smile, "for you may not have comprehended me fully, much like trying to grasp the experience of 'suchness' is akin to capturing the wind with your bare hands. You see, 'suchness' means wherever you stand, you are engaged in an intricate love affair with all that exists."

His words flowed like a soothing river, carrying an anecdote of acceptance and contentment. "There is no need to alter anyone or anything, and you need not transform yourself. Everything is precisely as it should be, a world that embodies perfection. This, my friend, is not a matter of belief, but of profound personal experience. It is not that I merely believe in it; I have lived it."

Emotion welled up within the king as he listened to these words, realising the depth of wisdom and enlightenment that this humble monk had attained.

Shambav said, "Belief is a state of mind, whereas faith is a state of being. Belief is borrowed, whereas faith is your own direct experience."

"Vidyaarthi," Shambav began, "Faith embodies both existence and experience in its essence. These two words hold profound significance for those who seek not to amass further knowledge or information but to embark on a profound transformation of their entire approach to existence. Faith simply is, as it stands, unburdened by external influences."

Harmony Amidst Diversity

"Amidst the chorus of nature's symphony, we learn that the richest treasures lie not in chasing illusions, but in embracing the beauty of what surrounds us."

- *Shree Shambav*

Once in a jungle not so far away, there resided a pair of crows named Camilla and Jones. Together, they had a lovely offspring named Kat. Kat was an inquisitive little crow, always bombarding her mother, Camilla, with many questions. Camilla, in turn, would provide her with thoughtful answers and praise her for being so clever.

Then one day, Kat's father, Jones, proposed, "How about we take a flight to the nearby town?"

Kat's eyes sparkled with excitement as she replied, "That sounds like a great idea! When should we embark on our journey?"

Jones decided, "Right now, this very instant!"

Kat's face beamed with joy, and she inquired, "Mom, have you ever been to the town?"

Camilla chuckled and responded, "We used to reside in the town once, but because of excessive noise and pollution, we made our home here in the jungle."

Their journey began shortly thereafter. While on the way, Kat noticed a massive gathering and festive celebration.

Curiously, Kat asked, "Mother, why are there so many people gathered in one place?"

Camilla explained, "They have gathered to celebrate the birth of a baby in a wealthy family."

Kat inquired, “Wealthy?”

Camilla confirmed, “Yes, dear.”

Continuing their journey, Kat spotted a smaller gathering with people rejoicing. She questioned, “Why is there a celebration at this gathering, Mother?”

Camilla replied, “It’s because a child was born into a less fortunate family.”

Kat further inquired, “Less fortunate?”

As they continued their journey, they came across a long procession accompanied by drumbeats and fireworks.

Kat, intrigued, inquired, “Mother, what is the purpose of this procession?”

Camilla replied, “It’s the funeral procession of a wealthy landlord.”

Shortly after, Kat noticed four individuals hurrying while carrying a deceased person. She immediately questioned, “Mother, why are there no people around this deceased person?”

Camilla explained, “He was a poor farmer.”

Kat wondered, “Mother, is it wrong to be born into a poor family?”

Jones, with a chuckle, interjected, "No, my dear. It is not about how you are born, but it is about how you live."

Kat persisted, her curiosity deepening. "Why does every living being have to face death?"

Jones, wearing a gentle smile, responded, "Kat, imagine a world where there was no death for living beings. In such a world, everyone might start to believe they are like gods, and the concept of a Supreme being might fade into oblivion."

Jones continued, his voice filled with wisdom, "Kat, the gatherings and rituals during a person's birth showcase the family they are born into, while the gatherings and ceremonies during their death reflect the goodness and impact they had on society and the people around them."

With a tinge of sadness, Jones added, "It's disheartening, Kat, that the respect, presence, and kindness one truly deserves during their lifetime often only becomes apparent after their departure."

Camilla's smile widened as she wove a tale: "Let me share with you a story, Kat. Once upon a time, God chose to descend to the earthly realm. As he traversed through the world, He encountered a solemn funeral procession. Slowly but surely, God and the procession reached a tranquil graveyard. It was a place filled with mourning and praises for the departed soul. As the final rites concluded, one by one, the mourners began to depart. The spirit left behind couldn't help but feel perplexed."

She continued, "The spirit pondered, 'Now, I understand we arrive in this world alone, and we must depart from it alone as well.'"

With a knowing smile, Camilla illustrated the irony, "God observed this realisation in the spirit's eyes and contemplated silently. He mused that throughout his life, the spirit had rushed relentlessly to amass wealth, gather the world's comforts, acquire the softest beds for slumber, and seek fame and recognition. All this while, he had remained oblivious to the fact that, in the end, he would rest in an unmovable cradle."

God cast a contemplative gaze over the diverse graveyards, each reflecting the divisions humans had created based on colour, creed, practice, and religion. Perplexed, He couldn't fathom why such distinctions existed. His divine perspective saw no distinctions among the plants and animals; they coexisted harmoniously. "Why," He pondered, "had humans chosen to perceive differences where none truly existed?"

As He surveyed the various burial grounds, God continued to question the divisions that humanity had imposed upon themselves. He thought deeply, "I have never regarded them differently. Why do they perceive themselves as distinct?" Even in the solemn moments of the last rites, these disparities persisted. God wondered, "What kind of beings are they? Are they truly my reflections?"

A sense of heaviness weighed upon His divine heart. Even in their ultimate moments in the material world, humans clung to their rituals, their power struggles, their racial biases, and their religious divides. God sighed, acknowledging the complexities of human nature, and prepared to depart from this place, hoping that one day, His creations would embrace unity over division.

In the divine realm, a faint voice reached God's ears, and a spirit addressed Him with recognition, "I know you; you must be God."

God responded with a warm smile and a nod, his curiosity piqued. He gently asked, "Who are you?"

With a serene smile, the spirit replied, "Lord, until a few hours ago, I was known as a Landlord, but now I find myself adrift, not knowing who I truly am. Why have you led me to wander here without an obvious purpose?"

God's smile remained filled with understanding and compassion. He replied, "When there was a purpose for you to fulfil in the earthly realm, you spent your time amassing wealth and sometimes troubled the innocent. It's a reminder, my child, that the length of one's life is not what truly matters, but how one chooses to live it."

Another youthful spirit, still seeking wisdom, questioned, "God, I was content here in this realm. Why did you insist I descend to the earthly plane, knowing that my journey there might lead me astray, causing harm instead of good?"

God's smile held both warmth and sorrow as He responded, "I sent you to the earthly realm with riches so that you could bring happiness to those around you. Yet, you chose to amass more wealth, often at the expense of innocent people, causing them further suffering and pain."

Another inquisitive spirit dared to ask, "Why is there no celebration or gathering here in this realm?"

God's smile remained, "I sent you to this realm to create celebrations and bring forth peace, happiness, and bliss. Instead, under the guise of gatherings and celebrations, you divided people based on colour, creed, and religion."

A concerned female spirit couldn't help but murmur her thoughts to God, "I have suffered as a girl."

With profound understanding, God replied, "Had you been born a boy, you would have faced different hardships. Remember, it is not your gender that defines your path, but how you navigate life's challenges that truly matters."

Yet another spirit spoke out, his voice tinged with sorrow, "God, what wrong have I committed to lead such a miserable life on Earth?"

God's response carried both compassion and wisdom: "It is the desire and insatiable craving that leads to misery. You were discontent with everything you possessed, despite being born into a wealthy family, holding an influential position, and having a loving family. Your perpetual yearning for more led to your misery."

An elderly spirit, his eyes filled with longing for understanding, inquired, "One thing has always perplexed me, Lord. Why do you call away the virtuous souls prematurely, leaving sinners to reign over the materialistic world, causing chaos and suffering to the innocent?"

God's answer resonated with profound truth, "If good souls were allowed to linger on Earth for too long, even they would succumb to the temptations of sin. Their premature departure ensures that their goodness remains untainted and serves as a guiding light for others."

Amid this profound exchange, another spirit spoke up, his voice carrying the weight of centuries of human conflict and suffering. "God, you have blessed us with majestic mountains, meandering rivers, towering trees, exquisite flowers, delicate shrubs, bountiful fruits, gentle breezes, and the mesmerising stars above. Yet, why did you also sow the seeds of hatred among humans, dividing them based on colour, caste, creed, and religion?"

God's response was a poignant blend of remorse and contemplation. He fell silent for a few moments, and the weight of the question hung heavily in the air. Finally, he spoke, his voice tinged with sadness, "If indeed I had a hand in this division, then it must be a grave mistake on my part. Even gods, it seems, are not immune to erring."

In an unexpected turn, the spirits erupted into laughter, their celestial voices resonating with a newfound understanding of the complexities of the human experience.

Immediately, another soul awoke and exclaimed, "God, I strangled myself to death to avoid all this chaos and confusion on Earth."

With an unwavering expression, God responded firmly, "You, my spirit, chose the path of escape. I granted you the opportunity to traverse the earthly realm, to encounter the suffering and pain inflicted by your kind. Yet, you turned away from the challenges that were meant to shape your spirit. There is no honour in such a choice, and I am not inclined to engage with those who shy away from adversity."

With curiosity in its voice, a spirit inquired, "Every being experiences the cycle of life and death. Why are you exempt from death, God?"

God replied, his tone filled with wisdom, "Who told you that? Every time a benevolent act is performed in the earthly realm, I am reborn anew. Conversely, when a sinful deed occurs, I undergo a metaphorical death, burdened by the weight of sorrow and disappointment."

With these words, God departed, leaving behind a profound sense of understanding among the spirits.

In the cosy shade of a tree, Camilla's child Kat gazed upon the world with innocent wonder. Camilla, the wise mother crow, decided it was time to impart some profound wisdom to her beloved offspring.

With a motherly smile, she began, "My dearest Kat, this wondrous world we dwell in was gifted to us by the divine hand of God. He painted this canvas of existence with vibrant colours, and He bestowed every living being with the same sacred right to inhabit it. Yet, in our human-like greed, bound by desire and enticed by cravings, we've woven a tapestry of divisions among ourselves – divisions of colour, creed, wealth, and religion. We have forgotten the essence of life – to celebrate its beauty."

Camilla's words flowed like a gentle stream, rich with meaning. She continued, her voice filled with emotion, "Instead of revelling in the natural wonders around us, we often chase elusive dreams, like trying to catch the wind in our wings. But, my dear, the key to true happiness lies in contentment, kindness, and compassion. It is found in helping those in need and in the simple act of being polite and respectful to our fellow beings."

As Camilla spoke, the rustling leaves and the distant chirping of birds seemed to join in agreement, bearing witness to the profound truths she shared with her attentive child. The warmth of her wisdom enveloped Kat, leaving a lasting impression on the young crow's heart.

The Resilience of Kindness

"Adversity may sweep us away, but our unwavering acts of kindness are the anchors that keep us grounded, reminding us that even in the roughest seas, we can find our way back to hope."

- *Shree Shambav*

Once, in a time long ago, a wise man named Kushagra found himself deep within the heart of a dense, mysterious jungle. The dense foliage whispered ancient secrets, and the forest floor crunched beneath his every step. As he ventured further into the enigmatic abyss, a distant cry reached his ears. The mournful sound tugged at his heart, compelling him to seek its source.

Kushagra followed the haunting cry through the tangled undergrowth until he came upon a woman, her face contorted with grief, sobbing uncontrollably. He approached her with a voice as gentle as the breeze rustling through the leaves and asked, "Why are you alone here? What has brought you to this desolate place, burdened with sorrow?"

The lady, her name is Kausalya, looked up through tear-streaked eyes and said, "I am alone and helpless. My family, who once cherished me, now considers me a burden. My story is one of happiness turned to despair."

Kausalya began her heartbreaking tale. She hailed from a wealthy merchant family, blessed with a loving husband and two children. Their life was a tapestry woven with happiness and generosity. Kausalya had a deep compassion for her fellow beings, helping the needy, supporting the helpless, and offering solace during times of adversity. Her husband had been her partner in this noble endeavour.

However, their idyllic life unravelled when her husband passed away. Her children, tainted by greed, began to resent her charitable actions. They went from grumbling about her deeds to forcing her to stop helping others. One fateful day, they cast her out, declaring that her presence in the household would lead them to poverty.

Homeless and heartbroken, the very people she had assisted in their times of need turned their backs on her, some even mocking her misfortune. Kausalya, after enduring immense suffering, found herself in the depths of this unforgiving jungle, contemplating the bleakness of her future.

Kushagra extended kindness to Kausalya, offering her sustenance and a place to rest. After a few hours, Kausalya woke and asked with a heavy heart, "'Why, oh why,' Why does my benevolence, my kindness, mark me as an innocent or a fool? Why is it that being good seems to invite nothing but pain, trouble, and suffering into my life? Have the kindness, generosity, and goodness I've held dear for so long been naught but tools for my people to exploit?"

Her eyes glistened with unshed tears, and her words carried the weight of a lifetime of hurt and confusion. Her story was one of innocence tarnished by betrayal, a tale that echoed the age-old struggle between the goodness of the heart and the callousness of the world.

Kushagra's eyes, like windows to a timeless wellspring of wisdom, glistened with a profound understanding of the human spirit. He leaned in closer to Kausalya, his words flowing like a gentle river, carrying both solace and insight.

Kushagra said, "Good people are akin to candles in the world's darkness. They willingly burn, casting their warm light to dispel the shadows. Even if their sacrifice remains unnoticed or, worse, is purposefully extinguished by the winds of ingratitude, it is not in vain. Dear Kausalya, your acts of kindness and your generosity create an exquisite energy field around you, much like a radiant halo. Like a candle's steady flame, your kindness weaves an intricate, invisible tapestry around you, a field of energy so pure and radiant that it has the power to draw positivity to your life, much like the stars are drawn to the night sky."

Kushagra's words were like a lifeline thrown to a drowning soul, an eloquent reminder that even in the face of the darkest storm, the candle of one's kindness can still light the way.

Tears welled up in Kausalya's eyes, her voice quivering as she poured her heart out, "All I have ever known in return for my goodness is an endless cycle of pain, suffering, losses, and nights filled with sleepless anguish."

Kushagra's response was a soothing balm to her wounded spirit. With a tenderness that seemed to transcend mere words, he said, "The investment of goodness, compassion, and kindness is the rare currency that never devalues, Kausalya. It's akin to the gentle fragrance of a flower, carrying its sweetness in every direction, gracing all who come into its embrace. Sometimes, the world may be slow to recognise its worth, but be assured, it does not go unnoticed by the universe."

Kushagra's words flowed like a soothing river, carrying both wisdom and solace. "Kausalya," he began, "you may question the duration of your endurance, and why you should continue to nurture kindness amidst the trials of life. But consider this: your good deeds are like the gentle ripples in a pond, creating an aura of positive energy that radiates far beyond what your eyes can perceive."

He leaned in, his eyes alight with the magic of storytelling. Kushagra said, "A tiny seed that finds its home in the rich soil of a forest floor. In the beginning, it may appear as though the world has forgotten it, hidden beneath the canopy of towering trees. Yet, over time, that little seed becomes a mighty tree, offering shade, shelter, and nourishment to countless creatures."

Kushagra's voice lowered to a conspiratorial whisper as if he were sharing the forest's secrets. "You, Kausalya, are much like that seed. Your kindness, your inherent goodness, may seem unseen or undervalued, but it is planting the seeds of change in the hearts of those you touch.

Let me share with you a small tale, a glimpse into the intricacies of our shared existence. In the heart of a dense forest, there lies a river. This river, like you, knows not haste or greed. It flows gently, nurturing the land it touches, providing sustenance and life to all who dwell by its banks. It asks for nothing in return but graces everything it encounters with the pure essence of its existence."

Kushagra gestured to the surrounding flora and fauna. "Observe the world around us, Kausalya. The trees offer their shade to weary travellers, the flowers bestow their beauty to all who pass, and the birds sing their songs for the joy of it, never seeking immediate rewards. Nature's generosity, its willingness to give without expectation, is your kin, your mentor, your silent companion in the grand symphony of life."

Kushagra said, "Just look around – in the grand tapestry of nature, everything gives without an immediate demand for returns, yet life flourishes and blossoms in abundance."

Kushagra embarked on another tale. Kushagra said, "In a tranquil village nestled beside a gentle river, surrounded by nature's lush embrace. In the heart of this village lived a young man named Ram, a living embodiment of generosity and kindness. His very existence seemed interwoven with the rhythms of Mother Nature herself, and he held a profound connection with the creatures that danced within her embrace."

One fateful day, as Ram wandered through the woods, he stumbled upon a wounded, fragile puppy that had strayed from its path, its eyes reflecting a world of lost innocence. Ram, like a compassionate guardian of souls, scooped up the fragile creature, cradling it in his arms. He brought the injured soul to his humble abode, nursing it back to health with a tenderness that likened him to a masterful healer. Their bond, akin to the unspoken language of the earth, deepened with each passing day, as their spirits intertwined like vines in a lush forest.

Then, as life often unfolds, tragedy descends upon the village like a relentless storm, leaving destruction in its wake. The tempest raged, swallowing homes and lives in its fury. Ram's family, like countless others, sought refuge on a nearby hill, forced to abandon their cherished homes. When the storm had exhausted its wrath and the villagers returned, grief clouded the air as many lives remained unaccounted for, lost to the torrents. The once-vibrant village was reduced to a landscape of desolation.

Ram, too, appeared to have been swept away by the relentless floodwaters. His parents, their hearts heavy with sorrow, clung to memories and mourned the loss of their beloved son.

But in the midst of the relentless storm, there was a solitary source of hope. The faithful puppy, her eyes brimming with tears that mirrored the grief of the village, refused to relinquish faith. With a determination as unyielding as a river's current, she continued to bark insistently, a siren of resilience amid desolation. Her unwavering devotion guided the villagers to a small opening in the earth, a fragile glimmer of hope amidst the darkness.

As the villagers dug fervently, their efforts akin to the determined roots of a tree that clung to the earth, they unearthed Ram, unconscious but alive. It was a moment that spoke of rebirth, like the first bud of a flower breaking through the frozen ground of spring.

Kushagra said, "In life, we are often swept away by the storms of adversity. But even when all seems lost, our unwavering acts of kindness and our bonds with others can act as beacons of hope, guiding us back to the surface when we are buried in despair."

Kushagra concluded, "When adversity befalls us, we discover the hidden facets of life. Ram's kindness and generosity saved him. Every painful experience in life is like charred ground that, in time, becomes green and filled with life again. We must move forward, like a river that only flows in one direction, confident in our journey and ready to face the challenges with strength and dignity."

With a compassionate smile, Kushagra emphasized, "Life is an echo. The good you spread will always come back to you. So, go out and do good, for that is the true measure of success."

The Search for the Formless Divine

"The quest to see God is a journey inward, where the heart serves as the compass to the divine's omnipresence."

- *Shree Shambav*

Long ago, in an era shrouded in the mists of time, a young boy named Nikash embarked on a relentless quest for the divine. He journeyed through treacherous terrains, scaling formidable mountains, traversing roaring rivers, and venturing deep into the heart of ancient forests. He sought answers from wise sages, visited sacred places, and even ventured into graveyards, all in pursuit of a singular goal—encountering God.

Years turned into decades as Nikash continued his unyielding search. With each step, he offered every part of himself, dedicating his very life to pursuing God's presence. Sacrificing the comfort of his parents, bidding farewell to his beloved childhood home, and relinquishing the bonds of friendship, family, and kin, he poured his heart into this pursuit, for he yearned for a divine revelation that transcended all else.

Yet, as time wore on, Nikash's spirit began to wane, and the flame of hope flickered in the face of what seemed like an unattainable dream. Wearied and disheartened, he found himself under the expansive shade of an ancient banyan tree, tears of desperation blurring his vision. His plea, spoken in whispers to the ether, was tinged with sorrow and despair. "God, please hear me," he implored. "How do you look? If you do not answer, I fear I will end my life without ever laying eyes upon you."

In that moment of vulnerability, as Nikash's tearful supplication hung in the air, a voice broke the silence, like a gentle breeze rustling through the leaves of the banyan tree. "Young man, why do you appear so troubled? It is evident that you are in the midst of a profound search."

Nikash opened his eyes to find an elderly man with a radiant smile gazing at him. With gratitude in his voice, Nikash spoke, "Master, I have dedicated countless years to the pursuit of God. Even after my most intense efforts, I have not been graced with a glimpse of the divine. My sole purpose in life is to find God."

He continued, his voice heavy with the weight of his sacrifice, "I have sacrificed my parents, my cherished home, my dearest friends, and my closest relatives, all in the name of this quest. Yet, now, I am left with nothing, not even a glimpse of God."

Siddharth, the elderly sage, offered a warm and knowing smile, "So, you seek God."

Nikash nodded solemnly, "Yes, master."

Siddharth's eyes seemed to twinkle with the wisdom of ages as he spoke, "God is not confined to any single form or place. He is omnipresent, omnipotent, and omniscient."

Nikash was intrigued by this revelation, "Everywhere?"

With a profound nod, Siddharth continued, "Indeed. God resides in every corner of the universe, in everything that exists. He resides within you, within me, within this banyan tree, in the leaves that rustle above us, in the flowing river nearby, in the buzzing bees, the song of the birds, and the vibrant dance of the flowers. He resides in the majesty of the mountains, in the warmth of the sun, the coolness of the moon, and the distant sparkle of the stars."

Nikash was both inspired and confused, "If God is truly everywhere, why have I not been able to see Him?"

Siddharth, with a knowing look, replied, "Let me share a story that might shed light on your quest. The studio was a sanctuary of dimly lit solitude. Within its walls, a sculptor stood before a block of stone, its surface as rugged and unyielding as the world's expectations. With a touch of reverence, the sculptor traced his fingers along the cool, unforgiving surface, contemplating the monumental task before him. He had been entrusted with a sacred duty—to carve an image of God.

As he ran his calloused fingers over the rough stone, his thoughts embarked on a journey into the realms of metaphysical contemplation. How could one encapsulate the divine within the confines of rock and chisel? How could a solitary form ever hope to capture the boundless essence of God?

The sculptor's mind became a labyrinth of metaphors and anecdotes, each path leading to a different interpretation of divinity. If he were to carve a plant, he would exclude the grace of animals and the complexity of humans. An animal would bypass the intricate nature of humankind and the tranquil beauty of plants. A human figure would leave out the creatures of the earth and the vibrant flora. Male or female, each form seemed to impose a limitation, locking away some facet of existence.

In the sculptor's heart, a profound revelation began to take shape, like a delicate lotus unfurling amidst a sea of metaphysical musings. God, he realised, transcended the constraints of form. God was the container for all forms, encompassing every facet of existence. In this transformative insight, he understood that the only way to create a vessel for the infinite was to carve no specific form at all.

Overwhelmed by the profundity of his epiphany, the sculptor chose not to chisel a particular figure. He sensed the weight of the divine presence within the unshaped stone and comprehended that the intangible essence of God could never be fully captured in a tangible form. Instead, he left the stone as it was, its rough and unshaped surface a symbol of the formless, a representation of the vastness of the divine.

The sculptor bowed before the uncarved stone, recognising it as the Linga—a symbol of the form of the formless. He whispered "OM Shambavism," a sacred chant that resonated through the studio, filling the space with a profound sense of peace and unity with the boundless cosmic consciousness. The sculptor had realised that sometimes, in the absence of physical form, the most profound expressions of divinity could be found.

Siddharth's voice was imbued with deep wisdom as he concluded, "Nikash, you can see and realise God when you become selfless, kind, and compassionate toward your fellow beings."

The young seeker felt a profound shift within himself, a realisation that the quest for God was not confined to an external journey but a transformation of the heart. Nikash saw the wisdom in Siddharth's words, understanding that true divinity existed in the way he lived his life and treated those around him.

With a newfound purpose, Nikash was determined to embody the qualities that would lead him to the divine. The years of relentless searching had transformed into a spiritual awakening. As he and Siddharth parted ways, a radiant smile adorned Nikash's face, much like the blossoming of a lotus amidst the chaos of his quest.

Throughout his life, Nikash found that the truest path to God was paved with selflessness, kindness, and compassion. He dedicated himself to these virtues, touching the lives of countless individuals with his boundless love and care.

The Tree of Friendship

"In the treasure troves of life, it's the beauty of bonds that transcends wealth and possessions."

- *Shree Shambav*

Long ago, Shree Shambav and his group of devotees found themselves strolling along the tranquil banks of a winding river. Among these devotees was a curious soul named Aarush, who, driven by a profound question, approached their guru.

Aarush inquired, “Guruji, what is the true essence of friendship?”

Shree Shambav, with a gentle smile and a heart filled with wisdom, replied, “Friendship, my dear Aarush, is a sacred bond. It is a state of enduring affection, unwavering esteem, profound intimacy, and unshakeable trust between two people. Regardless of cultural boundaries, friendships are the threads that weave the beautiful tapestry of a person’s life.”

With curiosity gleaming in his eyes, Aarush delved deeper, “But Guruji, why do we need friendship in our lives?”

Shree Shambav’s voice resonated as he responded, “Friendship holds the key to many doors in our lives. It offers us a sense of belonging, bolsters our confidence and self-esteem, acts as a shield against the storms of life, and safeguards us from the pitfalls of isolation and loneliness. True friends teach us, they expand the horizons of our perspective, provide solace in times of grief, offer emotional support when we are low, inspire us to reach for our dreams, introduce laughter into our days, and sometimes, guide us to leave behind unhealthy habits."

Aarush pondered for a moment and asked, "Guruji, is it important to have many friends?"

Shree Shambav, with a serene gaze, advised, "The number of friends is not the essence; the quality of your friendships holds the true value. It's about forming deep, meaningful connections with those who touch your heart and enrich your life."

Continuing, Shree Shambav elaborated, "True friendships are like ancient trees, meant to endure the test of time. They ask for sacrifice and support, and one must be willing to offer these when nurturing and preserving such cherished bonds."

Aarush, still eager to learn, questioned, "How can one differentiate between a good friend and a bad friend?"

Shree Shambav, his eyes twinkling with a knowing smile, shared an insightful story: "In a bygone era, there lived an aged man, feeble and frail, burdened by worry for his two sons. As he neared the end of his journey, he called his sons to his side for one final lesson. He requested each of them to bring a piece of coal and a piece of sandalwood."

One son promptly brought a piece of coal, while the other fetched a fragrant piece of sandalwood. The sons stood before their father, each holding their offering. The old man instructed them to drop to the ground and wash their hands, watching as they did so.

The son who held the sandalwood quickly responded, saying, “My hands are clean, and the aroma of the sandalwood still lingers.”

However, the other son, who had held the coal, said, “Even after washing my hands, I can still see traces of soot and feel the lingering darkness.”

The wise old man, with a serene yet firm demeanour, explained, “My sons, the company you keep in life is akin to the pieces of coal and sandalwood. Those who surround you can either cleanse your spirit like sandalwood, leaving behind a fragrance of positivity, or they can leave behind the dark smudges of negativity, like coal. The choice is yours, for the companions you choose will shape your path.”

Aarush, enlightened by this story, wondered, “Can good friends truly make a significant impact on our lives?”

Shree Shambav responded with profound insight and warmth, “Indeed, my dear Aarush, allow me to share another tale. Long ago, nestled in the embrace of a magnificent mango tree, a group of children found refuge beneath its sprawling canopy. They climbed its branches, plucking sweet mangoes, played amidst its lush sanctuary, and discovered solace in its nurturing shade. Among these children was a boy named Pratham, whose heart intertwined with the very soul of the tree."

Their friendship blossomed like the roots of an ancient tree, delving deeper with each passing year. As the boy grew, life's demands pulled him away, and the tree stood, silently yearning for his return. Days turned into years, marked by the tree's wistful musings and memories of days filled with laughter and shared secrets.

One day, Pratham returned to the tree, but his face bore a heavy shadow of sadness. The tree, thrilled to see its dear friend, inquired, "Pratham, why do you appear so downcast? I expected joy to fill your heart."

Pratham, however, responded with a heavy heart, "I'm no longer a child, and I see others with toys and wealth. I have neither the toys to play with nor the means to get them."

The tree, in all its wisdom, reassured him, "Pratham, your concerns are needless. While I may lack riches, my bountiful mangoes can be collected and sold, granting you the means to chase your dreams."

Pratham's eyes lit up with gratitude, and he departed with a promise of hope.

Years passed, and Pratham returned as a grown man, burdened with the weight of responsibilities and the aspirations of adulthood. He explained, "I must provide shelter for my family. I need a house, and I shall build one."

The tree's leaves drooped, yet it extended an offer of goodwill, "You may take my branches to craft your dwelling, my friend."

Pratham built his home, his heart brimming with gratitude for the tree's support.

Time flowed like a relentless river, and Pratham did not return for many years. The tree stood alone, its heart heavy with longing and memories.

One day, Pratham reappeared, wearied by life's struggles. The tree, seeing his forlorn state, yearned to bring solace. "Come and play with me," it offered.

But Pratham, now a man burdened by responsibilities, replied sternly, "I have no time for play. I am not as carefree as you. My family's safety depends on me, and I must catch fish from the nearby sea to support them."

"Why not fish then?" the tree inquired.

Pratham responded, "I lack a boat, and my commitment to my family is unwavering."

With a gentle smile, the tree suggested, "Take my trunk to build your boat."

Pratham was overjoyed and left with the wood. However, many more years passed without his return.

Finally, aged and frail, Pratham returned to the tree. The tree, with its branches gone, could no longer provide mangoes, but it welcomed him with open arms.

"I have no teeth to eat," Pratham confessed.

The tree, with empathy, replied, "I have no fruit to give."

The tree continued, "I have no branches to climb or swing on. I've lost it all."

The tree whispered, "And I stand here, my dear friend, with my roots intact."

Pratham sighed, "I've lost my home, and my family's needs are great."

The tree, though diminished, sheltered him, offering a silent embrace.

With tears in his eyes, Pratham spoke with a heavy heart, "I have learned the beauty of a bond that transcends wealth and possessions. I seek a place to rest, where your love endures."

In silence, they sat together, two souls intertwined, finding solace in the enduring bond of their friendship.

Echoes of Resilience

"My life is a testament to the transformative power of words—each syllable a brushstroke on the canvas of resilience, painting a narrative of unwavering spirit."

- *Shree Shambav*

Once upon a time, in the heart of a dense jungle, the Daisy fox family revelled in happiness, their joy echoed in the playful antics of their curious young one, Bambi. Every query Bambi raised was met with patient answers from Daisy, the nurturing mother. One fateful day, during their routine hunt, they encountered a hare. In the pursuit of their prey, they celebrated their success, unaware that their world was about to be engulfed by a ruthless inferno.

As fire encircled the forest, panic ensued. Bambi, Daisy, and the father fox attempted to escape, but the relentless flames claimed Bambi's parents, leaving her alone and orphaned. The traumatic loss shattered Bambi, leaving her in a state of profound grief and confusion. Bereft of guidance, she wandered, the spark of life extinguished from her once-bright eyes.

In the depths of despair, an aged crow named Koronis observed the desolate young fox. Moved by compassion, Koronis approached Bambi, asking the question that echoed in the heavy silence of the jungle: "What makes you so profoundly sad?" The weight of Bambi's sorrow was palpable, her spirit crushed under the burden of grief. Unperturbed, Koronis decided to accompany Bambi, providing silent solace as they journeyed together until they reached a place where fate would unfold its next chapter.

Koronis persistently inquired, "Bambi, you're young and seem intelligent, yet there's a profound sadness about you." He continued, "Bambi, why are you alone? Where are your parents?"

After a prolonged silence, Bambi began to weep, expressing, "I've lost my dearest parents in the fire. They perished before my eyes, and I was powerless to assist them. I was the one who urged them to chase the hare. Now, I'm left alone—no one to talk to, no one to listen, no home, no one to care, no one to tell me stories. My existence itself feels like a curse. I long for the fire to consume me, to end my pain."

Upon hearing Bambi's heart-wrenching tale, Koronis offered solace, providing her with nourishment. With empathy, Koronis asked, "If you don't mind, can I be a part of your family?" Bambi, tears streaming down her face, simply nodded.

As darkness enveloped the surroundings, Koronis shared uplifting stories, bringing Bambi into a night of peaceful sleep. The next morning, Bambi felt a profound rejuvenation, perceiving dancing flowers, swaying branches, and melodious birdsong—all vibrant signs of life. Observing Bambi's transformation, Koronis spoke gently, "Today, I want you to accompany you to the nearest deep jungle."

Bambi's excitement radiated as they journeyed together, and amidst their travel, Koronis wove tales that captivated the young fox's imagination. Their path led them to a small hill behind a grand tree. Koronis directed Bambi's attention and said, "Bambi, look at that fox. Her name is Callie. Despite having only two legs, can't you see the radiance of happiness in her?"

Inquisitive and touched, Bambi questioned with a sense of despair, "But how can she thrive in such a condition? She can't walk or run, hunt for food, or she's vulnerable to attacks. Yet, she appears remarkably content. How is such happiness possible?"

Koronis smiled warmly and reassured, "Bambi, patience is the key; time has a way of unfolding answers to all your questions." As they stood together, a thunderous roar echoed through the air, accompanied by the rhythmic footsteps of a lion's pride approaching Callie.

Bambi, growing impatient and fearful, turned to Koronis, expressing concern, "We might have made a mistake coming here. We could be in danger from these lions. And what about Callie? She'll be defenceless against these formidable creatures."

With a serene demeanour, Koronis continued to smile and calmly said, "Bambi, just watch and observe..."

To Bambi's profound astonishment, the lion approached Callie and, in a display of unexpected gentleness, bowed its head with respect. The younger lions joined in, playfully engaging with Callie.

Astonishingly, they even brought her food before departing.

Overwhelmed with emotion, Bambi was moved to tears. Koronis, ever the wise companion, consoled her, saying, "Fear not, young one. The divine, the creator of all beings, has a grand plan for every creation. Just as you witnessed today, trust in the unfolding of life around you and have faith in the unseen path that lies ahead."

Guided by Koronis, Bambi approached Callies, eager to understand the mysteries that unfolded before her. As Koronis narrated the tale, Callies welcomed them with a warm smile.

"Bambi," Callies spoke with a pearl of serene wisdom, "Life, like an unpredictable tempest, sweeps us into moments that reshape not just our outward journey but the very core of our being. These incidents may scar the vessel we inhabit, yet beneath the surface, a profound transformation occurs. While the corporeal frame may bear marks of disfigurement, it's in the depths of the soul that an unparalleled metamorphosis takes place. These experiences shatter the boundaries of mere existence, revealing layers of resilience that redefine the essence within. In the crucible of such trials, I've discovered that words, seemingly intangible, possess the alchemical power to transmute wounds into wisdom and pain into purpose."

Callies shared her poignant life story, revealing the chapters of her past. "In a bygone era, we thrived as a harmonious joint family, finding joy in the simple abundance of life. Contentment was our wealth, and the food we received was a cause for celebration. One scorching summer day, as my family rested, I noticed a distant flicker—an ominous fire threatening our haven. Instinctively, I sprinted towards it, driven by the need to ensure the safety of the lion cubs.

Amidst the engulfing flames, I risked my life to rescue five precious cubs. However, in the process of saving the last one, a cruel twist of fate unfolded—a tree crashed onto my hind leg, robbing me of both. Despite the excruciating pain, the knowledge that I had preserved six lives filled my heart with profound happiness, and I succumbed to unconsciousness.

Days later, as I awoke from the depths of my unconscious state, I found myself encircled by the lion herd. Tears welled in their eyes, mirroring the emotional tumult within. The silent acknowledgement of my sacrifice spoke volumes, and in that moment, I understood the intricate tapestry of life's unpredictable threads."

Callies, her heart heavy with emotion, spoke, "I saved your cubs; there should be joy in your hearts. Why do I sense sadness?"

The lion, with a sombre nod, replied, "You rescued our family, but, alas, we couldn't rescue yours. We witnessed them succumb to the merciless flames."

A heavy silence settled over them. Callies, her voice trembling, inquired, "Are you saying I have no family left?"

The lion, drawing a deep breath, confessed, "No, Callies. I am your father, and Amara is your mother. They, along with the pride, are your family. You are the strength that stands as our hind legs. Forever indebted to your sacrifice, you are akin to a deity in our eyes, our saviour, tears reflecting the gratitude that words fail to convey."

Callie's voice resonated with pride, "I take pride in my actions, Bambi. Today, I have a large and loving family, and I find beauty in everything around me."

She continued, "Bambi, a few years back, fate wove a twist into my life—a chapter some might deem a tragedy. An accident altered my existence, leaving me with physical scars and a body that defied societal norms. The world, in its harsh judgment, cast me as a casualty and labelled me as disabled. Yet, within the crucible of adversity, I unearthed an extraordinary resilience that transcended the limitations of the physical."

In the tapestry of my journey, I stumbled upon a mentor, a beacon of wisdom named Amara—my mother. Her path bore the scars of challenges, and within her words, I discovered solace; within her perspective, a revelation echoed. She spoke, "Within every fracture, there resides an opportunity for transformation. It's not about the disability; it's about embracing your unique ability."

Callie reflected, "A pivotal chapter unfolded, not just redirecting my course, but moulding the essence of who I am."

Embracing the wisdom bestowed upon me, I gracefully navigated the intricate web of societal perceptions. I stood resilient, not as a victim, but as a living testament to the alchemical potency residing in each uttered syllable. My unwavering belief in the transformative power of words became the guiding light illuminating my path.

Every setback, every perceived limitation, transformed into a stepping stone, each bearing witness to the redefinition of strength. The physical deformity perceived by the world served merely as a canvas, a masterpiece of resilience painted stroke by stroke with vibrant hues of courage and an indomitable spirit.

In the face of adversity, I chose not to surrender but to metamorphose, transcending the label of disabled to embrace the identity of differently abled. The power inherent in words became my compass, steering me towards a narrative of empowerment. As I embraced this paradigm shift, the world bore witness not just to the trajectory of my physical journey but to the transformative odyssey of my soul.

Koronis spoke with profound wisdom, saying, “Bambi, the story of Callies unfolds as a symphony of experience, revealing the profound potency of words to heal, empower, and redefine. In the grand tapestry of existence, each word becomes a melody, resonating with the rhythm of resilience and strength.”

Callies said, “I stand not as a victim of circumstance but as a living testament to the transformative magic encapsulated in every uttered syllable. My belief in the power of words transcends societal labels, echoing in the symphony of strengths woven into the fabric of my being. Each word becomes a brushstroke, painting a narrative of courage, tenacity, and an unwavering spirit that defies the limitations of the physical realm, creating a masterpiece of resilience and empowerment.”

A Journey Through Valleys of Wisdom

"The search for a perfect master unveils not on majestic peaks but in the echoes of a simple dance, teaching that enlightenment resides in the rhythm of life."

- *Shree Shambav*

In the arduous quest for awakening, Shenzu, a weary young devotee, traversed diverse landscapes—forests, rivers, and valleys. Despite years of searching and meeting various masters, his journey seemed futile. Exhausted and on the verge of despair, he found himself wandering in the woods.

Amidst the deep shadows of the trees, Shenzu's prayers resonated with the stillness of nature. Suddenly, in the distance, a sight caught his eye—an old man, lost in a dance that seemed to echo with the rhythm of the universe. Intrigued and drawn by the apparent joy amidst the world's pain, Shenzu approached the old man with a yearning question, "What brings you such happiness amid the pain and suffering that surrounds us?"

The old man chuckled heartily and remarked, "Ah, young one, years in pursuit of a perfect master, and yet, clarity eludes you."

Shenzu, taken aback, inquired, "How do you know of my quest?"

The old man's smile deepened, "The winds carry whispers of seekers like you. If perfection is what you seek, climb the nearest towering mountain and seek out Jun."

Shenzu's heart brimmed with gratitude as he departed, leaving the old man in the serene woods. The path he embarked upon was a formidable ascent, its steepness echoing the challenges of his relentless pursuit. The terrain, harsh and unforgiving, mirrored the arduousness of his quest. Shivering in the cold, Shenzu battled the harsh elements, determined to find his newfound master.

The journey unfolded on a precipitous course, marked by icy winds and bone-chilling temperatures. As days turned into nights, Shenzu's resilience faced its sternest test. The mountain, stoic and silent, seemed to challenge the very essence of his pursuit. Fatigue took its toll, and Shenzu succumbed to illness, left alone in the wilderness under the watchful gaze of twinkling stars.

In the stillness of that frigid night, as clouds painted intricate patterns across the sky, Shenzu's mind became a canvas of questions. Why this desolate place for a master? What purpose lay hidden in this seemingly barren expanse? His contemplations ushered him into a deep slumber, where dreams and uncertainties intermingled.

The next day dawned with the sun casting its warm glow upon Shenzu, nestled atop the mountain. The dwindling food supply and the challenges of the journey failed to deter his spirit. With determination etched on his face, Shenzu resumed his ascent, eager to uncover the mysteries that awaited him at the mountain's zenith.

Finally, after an exhaustive climb, Shenzu reached the pinnacle. To his surprise, there was no one in sight. The winds whispered secrets, and the panoramic view unveiled a vast, untamed landscape. In the solitude of that mountaintop, Shenzu stood a lone seeker, wondering about the purpose of this pilgrimage and the absence of the master he sought.

In the wake of his arduous ascent and the disappointment of not finding the master he sought, Shenzu succumbed to exhaustion, collapsing under the weight of his weary journey. As he lay unconscious, time flowed in a liminal state, marked only by the subtle rustle of the mountain breeze and the distant whispers of nature.

In the hushed embrace of the mountain's solitude, Shenzu was roused from his unconsciousness by a gentle voice, a melodic cadence that cut through the stillness. "Wake up, young man," the voice urged, carrying with it a curiosity born of compassion. Slowly, Shenzu regained awareness, his eyes adjusting to the surrounding brilliance.

Before him stood an old man, draped in weathered cloth that mirrored the rugged landscape. His hair, dry and tousled, framed a face marked by the passage of time. A long beard flowed with quiet wisdom, and in his hand, a well-worn staff bore witness to the miles he had traversed. This elderly figure, a humble resident of the mountain, appeared frail, yet exuded an aura of resilience.

The old man extended an invitation, "Come to my humble hut nearby." Shenzu, still reeling from his exhaustion, mustered the strength to follow. The journey, albeit short, unfolded with deliberate steps, each one echoing the shared stories of those who had ventured to the heart of the mountain.

As Shenzu wearily followed, his curiosity lingered. The old man, Jun, seemed a far cry from the envisioned perfect master. In the modest hut, Jun, with an air of simplicity and grace, offered Shenzu a seat, a cup of steaming tea, and warm clothes, a balm for the physical toll exacted by the journey. The dim glow of the hearth cast flickering shadows, creating an ambience where time seemed to bend.

Shenzu, wrestling with the dissonance between expectation and reality, ventured, "Are you Jun?" The old man's eyes, carrying the weight of countless stories, crinkled in a smile as he confirmed, "Yes, I am Jun. Have you come to see me?"

In the ensuing days, Shenzu observed Jun engaging in the simple routines of life, a stark contrast to the anticipated profundity. Jun's actions mirrored those of any ordinary person, and the disquiet within Shenzu deepened. The dissonance between his quest for enlightenment and the ordinariness of Jun's existence became palpable.

One morning, as sunlight painted the mountain peaks, Shenzu, grappling with his internal turmoil, approached Jun with a heavy heart. "Jun, I am planning to return," he declared, a lamentation tinged with the echoes of unmet expectations.

Jun's laughter, echoing through the mountain air, was an unbridled expression of mirth. Shenzu, perplexed by this unexpected outburst, could only watch as Jun's laughter danced like a mountain stream, unrestrained and full of life. The old man's eyes twinkled with a knowing light, as if privy to a cosmic joke that eluded the weary seeker.

Amid his laughter, Jun posed a question, "Shenzu, why did you come here? What compels you to return?" Shenzu, disarmed by the candid inquiry, hesitated before responding, "Jun, I sought a perfect master to dispel my doubts. Yet, I find myself unable to locate one."

Jun's laughter, though softened, lingered in the air as he nodded thoughtfully. "A perfect master," he echoed, "and where, my friend, do you suppose you can find such a being?" Shenzu, standing at the crossroads of realisation, reiterated, "Yes, that is precisely what I seek."

With a calm that belied the weight of his words, Jun said, "The search for a perfect master is like chasing the wind. You may feel its presence, but grasping it remains elusive." Shenzu, his quest facing the inevitability of uncertainty, questioned, "Then where, Jun, can I find a master capable of answering my queries?"

Jun, his laughter subsiding, requested, "May I know the nature of your search?" Shenzu, now confronted with the need to articulate the essence of his relentless quest, gathered his thoughts and began to unveil the tapestry of his longing for wisdom and enlightenment.

Shenzu, standing on the precipice of his quest for enlightenment, couldn't contain the burning question within him. "How can one attain awakening, especially for those unfamiliar with the intricacies of consciousness?" he asked earnestly. Jun, the wise sage of the mountain, met Shenzu's inquiry with a knowing smile as if the question itself resonated with the echoes of countless seekers who had tread these paths before.

"Did you journey all the way here seeking an answer to this question?" Jun mused, his eyes reflecting the depth of insight that only a seasoned sage could possess. Shenzu, feeling the gravity of the quest he embarked upon, nodded in acknowledgement.

Jun, with an almost mischievous twinkle in his eye, continued, “In the valley below, an old man, who dances and sings, would have given you the answer.” Shenzu’s curiosity stirred, wondering if Jun spoke of the enigmatic old man he encountered amidst the whispering trees of the woods. The tendrils of mystery and revelation intertwined, urging Shenzu to explore the valleys that held the wisdom he sought.

Jun continued and said, “Let me narrate a story - a tale of two contrasting souls – Ezra and Silas. Ezra, a vivacious and beautiful soul, embodied a life unfettered by the chains of fear or the allure of distant heavens. He revelled in the present moment, finding joy in the simple pleasures of life. After a day's labour, he would immerse himself in the enchanting melodies of his musical instrument, dancing in the woods and strolling along the serene beach, savouring the tranquillity of the night.”

Silas, on the other hand, stood as a stark contrast. Despite his wealth and stature, he lived imprisoned in perpetual sadness. Bound by the chains of his thoughts, he remained confined to his workspace, a stranger to the laughter that eluded him, unable to appreciate the beauty that surrounded him. A silent envy lingered within Silas, watching Ezra, the servant, live a life akin to royalty, unburdened by the weight of tomorrow's uncertainties.

One fateful day, Ezra, noticing Silas's perpetual gloom, implored him to step out of the shadows and embrace the joy of the present moment. With unwavering enthusiasm, Ezra beckoned Silas to join him in cherishing the beauty of the world – the full-moon night, the azure sky, the twinkling stars, the whistling winds, and the dancing trees.

Resistant at first, Silas hesitated, clinging to the shackles of his thoughts. But Ezra, with a gentle force, pulled him into the garden of life. There, amidst the beauty of nature, Ezra began to dance, his balalaika resonating with a melody that echoed through the night. Witnessing Ezra's uninhibited dance and feeling the vibrant energy, Silas, for the first time, surrendered to the moment. He began to dance, too, and in that shared dance, he discovered the elixir of being truly alive.

Shenzu realised the depth of this transformative tale and conveyed a profound truth – that enlightenment lies not in the complexities of consciousness but in the simplicity of living fully in each moment.

To the young devotee Shenzu, the Jun whispered, "Listen to Ezra's story, for within it, you'll find the key to enlightenment – a dance with life, a celebration of the present, and an acknowledgement that, in every fleeting moment, the essence of being truly alive is discovered."

Resilience Unveiled

"In the tapestry of life, storms are not mere chaos; they are the masterful weavers of resilience, crafting threads of gratitude, joy, and strength in the soul's journey through the meadows of adversity."

- *Shree Shambav*

Shree Shambav and Oliver strolled through the meadows where they encountered a feeble and despondent man named John. Concerned, Oliver asked, "Why do you look so sad?"

Tears streamed down John's face, and Oliver persisted, "Why are you alone? What's making you feel so helpless?"

In a voice laden with sorrow, John replied, "How can I be happy? I've lost everything—my family, my home, all that I've earned over the years, and my friends. I am utterly alone. The storm took it all away."

Desperation lingered in his voice as he questioned, "How could I find happiness? My existence feels burdensome. I don't know what to do next."

After a prolonged silence, Shree Shambav suggested, "Have some food and rest for a while."

As the three of them continued wandering in the meadows, John began to share his story. "My name is John. I used to play in these meadows with my friends when I was young. Now, I've lost everyone." He pointed towards the other side and continued, "Look there, we've lost everything we've earned. The storm ruined our lives, our wealth, and my dear ones. I'm left worthless and lonely. I don't know why I exist. I don't know what to do next."

Curious about the why behind the suffering, Oliver turned to Shree Shambav. "Master, why must one endure so much suffering?"

Shree Shambav responded, "Oliver, let us learn the lessons the storms of life can teach us."

He began narrating a story about Ava, a woman from a coastal village, who faced the storms of life. Ava's parents passed away when she was young, and through hard work, she built a small business in her village. Love found hcr, and she got married.

Ava's odyssey unfolded with the arrival of a tempest—a fierce manifestation of nature's might that echoed the tumult within her own life. As the storm clouds gathered and the winds began to howl, however, a disastrous storm wiped away her entire village, leaving Ava alone on the shoreline, a solitary figure confronting the elemental fury. The tempest, an allegory for life's adversities, unleashed its relentless assault, leaving her drenched in the downpour of challenges.

"In the tapestry of her existence, storms were not just meteorological events; they were profound teachers, imparting lessons that went beyond the transient turbulence of the weather," Shree Shambav continued.

Amidst the chaos, Ava discerned the first lesson—the profound art of real gratitude. In the face of the storm's fury, she discovered a newfound appreciation for the simple shelter that shielded her from the tempest. The relentless winds whispered that gratitude is not a mere acknowledgement of blessings in fair weather but an acknowledgement that solace and appreciation can be found even amid chaos.

With each gust of wind and lash of rain, Ava learned the nuanced dance of real joy. Amidst the uproar of the storm, there existed a peculiar exhilaration, a celebration of resilience that revelled in finding beauty amid turmoil. Real joy, she realised, was not contingent upon the absence of challenges but manifested in the spirited dance in the rain, embracing life's turbulence with a courageous heart.

As the storm raged on, a moment of eerie calm enveloped the surroundings, unveiling the third lesson—real peace. In the eye of the storm, where chaos surrendered to serenity, Ava grasped that true peace is not the absence of storms, but the calmness that resides within, weathering all adversities with unwavering composure.

The tempest, unrelenting in its teachings, unfolded the concept of real treasure. In the debris left in its wake, Ava unearthed not material riches but the jewels of inner strength, resilience, and a profound understanding of what truly mattered in the grand tapestry of existence.

The tempest's fury sculpted the landscape of Ava's life, teaching her about real strength. Trees that bent but did not break, cliffs that withstood the pounding waves—they became symbols of enduring strength. The storm conveyed that real strength lies not in avoiding challenges but in standing tall and resolute in their midst.

In the aftermath of the storm, as the sun emerged from behind the retreating clouds, Ava discovered the essence of real faithfulness. Just as the sea faithfully embraced the shore after the tempest, she realised the power of unwavering commitment—be it to oneself, to others, or the arduous journey through life's storms.

With gratitude, joy, peace, treasure, strength, and faithfulness etched into the fibres of her being, Ava finally arrived at the last lesson—the concept of a real home. The storm had tested her roots, the foundations of her existence, and she discovered that home was not merely a physical space but the resilience of the heart, a sanctuary within that withstood the fiercest gales.

In the tranquil calm that followed, as the sun bathed the landscape in a warm, golden glow, Ava stood on the shore, transformed. The storm, once a harbinger of chaos, had become her greatest teacher. With a heart laden with the lessons of gratitude, joy, peace, treasure, strength, faithfulness, and the true meaning of home, Ava faced the horizon, ready for the next chapter of life's unpredictable journey. The storms had sculpted her into a tapestry of resilience, a living testament to the profound lessons only storms could teach.

As Ava stood transformed on the shore, the storm, once a harbinger of chaos, had become her greatest teacher.

Shree Shambav said, "In the tapestry of our existence, storms are more than just chaos; they are profound teachers, sculpting resilience from the wreckage of our trials. As Ava found strength in the storm's fury, may we embrace life's tempests, for within them lie the transformative lessons that weave the fabric of our deepest resilience?"

Returning to the present moment, Shree Shambav invited John to reflect on the parallels between Ava's journey and his own, asserting that the storms of life were potent teachers offering profound insights.

As they continued their walk, John, deep in contemplation, began to sense a glimmer of hope amid the ruins of his tempest. The meadows, once a witness to his sorrow, now bore witness to a silent transformation—a realisation that, just like Ava, he too could emerge from the storm, sculpted into a tapestry of resilience by life's invaluable lessons.

A Tapestry of Life's Triumphs

"The value of life is not measured in its length, but in the depth of experiences, the resilience we summon in storms, and the lasting impact we leave on the hearts of others."

- *Shree Shambav*

While traversing diverse landscapes, Shree Shambav and his devotees encountered poignant scenes that painted the contrasting hues of life. A young woman, a blend of disturbance and happiness, emerged from the primary health centre, clutching her husband's hands. They bowed their heads at the temple, expressing gratitude for the priceless gift of a new life. Days later, an aged couple celebrated their newborn grandchild, smiling and laughing, their joy echoing through the church's prayerful ambience.

However, amidst these moments of celebration, the travellers witnessed a middle-aged woman leaving the hospital, her eyes filled with tears, her face wrinkled with despair. Later, her husband's lifeless body, wrapped in white cloth, lay peacefully on a stretcher. Clinging to his hands for the last time, she bowed before the temple, tears silently tracing her cheeks.

Amidst these scenes of joy and sorrow, Liam grappled with the unsettling realities of life and death. He contemplated the cyclical nature of existence, where we commence our journey with a cry, extend heartfelt welcomes, and conclude with tears. In the transient moments, we carve an identity known as 'Me.'

Liam, disturbed by the belief in an endless journey in this earthly realm, confronted the reality that life follows a wheel-like pattern. Every birth shadows an impending death, and every death heralds a new birth. Despite achievements or losses, hatred or love, everybody eventually returns to the earth, leaving behind the tears of beloved ones. Yet, life persists, and the world continues in its usual rhythm.

Perturbed by these reflections, Liam sought answers, questioning the value of life. The irritable question gnawed at him, making him restless. He turned to Shree Shambav and asked, "Master, what is the value of life? After witnessing myriad incidents in the last few days."

Shree Shambav's eyes sparkled with a knowing twinkle as he began, "Allow me to weave a tale, a tale of resilience and untamed spirit. In the heart of a quiet village, cradled by mist-kissed mountains, lived a young girl named Maya. Her laughter echoed through the village, and her curiosity was a force that set her apart. Yet, Maya viewed life through a lens unseen by others, a lens that revealed the intricate threads of the human experience—a tale both stormy and tender, much like a blossoming flower in the tempest."

Maya's roots were not entwined with privilege. Her upbringing occurred in a world that habitually underestimated the potential of women, confining them to roles of subdued submission. But Maya stood distinct. From the earliest whispers of her youth, an internal fire blazed within her—a spirit akin to a phoenix, defiantly yearning to ascend from the ashes.

As a child, Maya sought refuge in the sanctuary of a hidden grove on the village's outskirts. There, beneath the sheltering embrace of ancient trees, she wove dreams that transcended the societal confines enclosing her. In the tapestry of her imagination, she envisioned herself as a beacon of change, an indomitable force to be reckoned with, and a wellspring of inspiration for generations yet unborn.

Maya's journey unfolded amidst the formidable obstacles. When her fervent desire to learn found a voice, village elders scorned the idea, their voices dripping with condescension. "Women belong in the home," they asserted. Undeterred, Maya's determination proved unyielding. She sought out a benevolent old scholar, a custodian of wisdom, who recognised the flame burning in her eyes. Under his guidance, she delved into the mysteries of the written word and the vast universe.

Maya's story, a testament to resilience, unfolded in the quiet village, revealing a spirit unbound by societal expectations. Shree Shambav continued, "Maya's journey is a symphony of the indomitable human spirit, a melody that echoes the strength of a storm and the delicate grace of a flower. Let her tale inspire the fires within, the ones that refuse to be extinguished by the winds of adversity."

One sunlit morning, as Maya wandered through the enchanting woods, she stumbled upon an old monk seated near a glistening pond. His face radiated a serene depth, and his eyes sparkled with a wisdom accumulated through the ages. The air hung heavy with the profound silence that surrounded the monk.

The old monk, acknowledging Maya's presence, greeted her with a warm smile and inquired, "What brings you to these deep woods, young child?"

Maya, captivated by the monk's aura of tranquillity, replied, "I have journeyed far to contemplate the beauty of nature and to unravel the true meaning of life."

The old monk, still smiling, imparted his wisdom, "Life is a precious gift, and each moment holds immense value."

Perplexed, Maya questioned, "Precious gift?"

With a nod of his head, the old monk continued, "Allow me to share a story." He began recounting a tale of a tiny seed, uncertain of its purpose, encountering adversity in harsh weather, darkness, and pain. Yet, it persevered, eagerly awaiting nourishment, water, and the struggle to reach sunlight. Over time, this seemingly insignificant seed transformed into a majestic tree, providing shade, shelter, nourishment to hungry birds, and beauty to all around—a living testament to life's journey.

"Dear Maya," the old monk gently said, "like that tiny seed, life begins small, filled with uncertainty and challenges. Yet, with resilience and perseverance, it grows into something magnificent, touching the lives of others."

Maya, deep in thought, realised the profound truth in the monk's words. "We are all like seeds," she declared.

The old monk affirmed, "Yes, each one of us has the potential to grow and make a difference, to spread joy and love in the world. That is the true value of life."

From that moment, Maya embraced every passing moment with gratitude and purpose. She shared her infectious laughter, offered help to those around her, and revelled in the simple joys of life. Recognising that the value of life lay not in its length but in the depth of experiences and their impact on others, Maya evolved into a compassionate, kind, and wise young woman.

Years passed, and Maya's influence rippled through the lives of those she touched. Wherever she went, she brought smiles and happiness, embodying the true value of life. Her journey, akin to the tiny seed, blossomed into something remarkable—a legacy of love and inspiration that echoed through time, a reminder that the essence of life lies in how deeply one touches the hearts of others.

As the old monk had foreseen, Maya's life unfolded like a beautifully bloomed flower, leaving an indelible mark on the world—a testament to the enduring significance of embracing life's journey with resilience, purpose, and a heart full of love.

As the years unfolded, Maya's reservoir of knowledge strengthened into a radiant guiding light for her community. She devoted herself to sharing wisdom with children, encouraging them to dream beyond the confines of societal norms. Through her teachings, she ignited a flame, akin to the one that had driven her to triumph over adversity.

Yet, life, in its unpredictable course, has a way of testing even the most resilient spirits. A calamity descended upon the village—a devastating storm that left homes in ruins and hearts shrouded in despair. In the aftermath, Maya emerged as a formidable pillar of strength. With unwavering resolve, she rallied the villagers, orchestrating relief efforts and spearheading the reconstruction of shattered homes. Her hands, once delicate, now bore the calluses of unyielding resilience.

However, Maya's most profound test awaited her. Fate, in its inscrutable design, dealt her a personal blow. A ferocious fire engulfed her cherished home, reducing the once-vibrant grove to smouldering ruins. As Maya gazed upon the remnants of her past, tears streamed down her face. It seemed as if the universe itself was scrutinising the depths of her spirit.

Yet, in that poignant moment of desolation, Maya unearthed her true strength. With an unwavering determination, she embarked on a mission to transform the scorched earth into a symbol of hope. Each seed she planted served as a testament to her unyielding spirit. And as the first buds of green emerged from the blackened soil, Maya stood tall, her heart resonating with the triumphant cry of a phoenix taking flight.

The news of Maya's resilience echoed far and wide, reaching the ears of those who had once doubted her. The village, once confining her, now drew inspiration from her indomitable will. Maya's journey, marked by hardship and transformation, became a luminous beacon of empowerment—a poignant reminder that the resilience of women, akin to the phoenix, allows them to rise from the ashes of despair and soar to new heights, illuminating the world with their brilliance.

Shree Shambav, reflecting on Maya's story, asserted, "Maya's journey is not merely one of survival; it is a testament to the boundless capacity of the human spirit to overcome adversity and emerge stronger than ever before. It speaks to the indomitable resilience of women, who, like the phoenix, can ascend from the ashes of despair, igniting change and setting the world ablaze with their boundless potential."

In the heart of that village, Maya's legacy persisted—a poignant reminder to all that a woman's strength is comparable to that of a phoenix, fierce and unyielding, capable of sparking change and setting the world ablaze with her limitless potential.

Shree Shambav said, "In the tapestry of life, hardship and resilience are the threads that weave the most profound stories. Maya's journey, a testament to the strength within, teaches us that from the ashes of despair, the phoenix of the human spirit can ascend, illuminating the world with the brilliance of boundless potential. Life's beauty lies not just in joyous moments but in the triumphant rise from the depths of adversity, for therein lies the priceless essence of our shared journey."

Shree Shambav, addressing Liam, imparted his wisdom, "Life is a beautiful journey, Liam. Embrace it in all its facets, for it is priceless. Every moment of suffering, every pang of pain, every flicker of happiness, and every shroud of sadness—all are integral parts of our unique journey. Accept life as it unfolds, for, indeed, life is beautiful."

A Journey Through Suffering's Tapestry

"Embrace your scars, for in the wounded chapters of your existence, you'll find the ink that writes the most profound stories of strength and transformation."

- *Shree Shambav*

In the tapestry of existence, where lives intersect like threads woven into intricate patterns, Shree Shambav and his band of devotees embarked on a journey that revealed the myriad faces of suffering. As they traversed diverse landscapes, they witnessed the silent struggles that defined human existence.

While wandering through a bustling market square, the entourage chanced upon a woman whose tear-streaked cheeks betrayed a profound ache emanating from the depths of her soul. When approached, she shared her silent lament – a yearning for the laughter of children, an unfulfilled desire to cradle her offspring. Her sorrow resonated like a poignant melody, seemingly in harmony with the very pulse of the universe.

Not far away, another scene unfolded – a mother, weathered by life's storms, cradled a feverish child in her arms, the vulnerability of youth stark against the backdrop of worldly challenges. Her worry was palpable, a testament to the lengths a parent would go to shield their progeny from the harsh winds of existence.

On this journey, the gaze of Shree Shambav's disciple, Adhrit, became a mirror reflecting the profound diversity of human suffering. Touched by the myriad stories, he posed a question that echoed through the group's contemplative silence.

Adhrit, the inquisitive seeker among Shree Shambav's disciples, found himself entangled in contemplation. Amidst such diverse suffering, questions danced on the tip of his tongue. "Master," he queried, "are these trials not avoidable? Can one truly be free from the chains of suffering?"

Shree Shambav, with a gaze that held the weight of eternity, responded, "Suffering, my dear Adhrit, is the silent companion of every soul. Rich or poor, healthy or ailing, each bears the burdens of their unique journey. It is an intrinsic part of existence, a thread woven into the very fabric of life."

As the journey unfolded, Shree Shambav took the opportunity to delve into the essence of suffering, unravelling the intricate threads that wove the fabric of human despair. His words, like a gentle breeze guiding a lost traveller, carried profound truths.

"Suffering arises," Shree Shambav explained, "from our refusal to acknowledge our divine nature, our failure to appreciate the interconnectedness of all things, our resistance to the impermanence of life, and our attachments to transient comforts."

He continued, "True wholeness emerges from embracing all facets of ourselves, acknowledging our connection to the cosmos. Our suffering, though omnipresent, can become a catalyst for transformation when offered to a cause greater than ourselves."

In a different chapter of their journey, the group encountered a wealthy merchant, burdened by a profound discontent with the opulence of his surroundings. His wealth, instead of bestowing joy, became a heavy yoke, chaining him to a life devoid of true fulfilment.

As Adhrit observed these diverse stories unfold, he couldn't help but ponder, "Can we break free from the relentless grip of suffering?"

Shree Shambav's response was laden with profound insights. "Understanding the roots of our suffering is the first step," he explained. "It stems from resistance to impermanence, the illusion of separation, clinging to identity, and yearning for a reality different from what is. By accepting impermanence and connecting with our intrinsic nature, we transform suffering into awareness, finding peace and happiness."

Shree Shambav said, "Adhrit, let me narrate a story. Once upon a time, in a small village nestled between rolling hills, there lived a woman named Calista. Calista's life was a tapestry woven with threads of joy and sorrow, but it was the latter that left an indelible mark on her soul."

Calista, a kind-hearted soul, had faced her fair share of tribulations. From the loss of loved ones to the trials of poverty, life had sculpted her with the chisel of suffering. Yet, in the crucible of hardship, Calista discovered the alchemy of resilience and compassion.

One day, as Calista strolled through the village, she noticed a young mother, tears glistening in her eyes. The woman, burdened by the weight of a sick child, felt the piercing arrows of suffering. Calista approached, offering a comforting embrace and words of solace. In that moment, she transformed the shared pain into a bridge of empathy.

Walking further, Calista encountered a man of wealth, adorned in silken garments, his countenance clouded with discontent. Intrigued, she engaged him in conversation. The man revealed the ache within his heart, the emptiness that no riches could fill. Calista, with gentle words, unravelled the layers of his suffering, imparting the wisdom that happiness blossoms not from wealth, but from the richness of the soul.

As the sun dipped below the horizon, casting long shadows over the village, Calista's journey continued. She encountered the struggles of a father fretting over his child's education, a woman yearning for the blessing of motherhood, and an elder grappling with the solitude of old age. To each, Calista became a compassionate companion, sharing the burden of their suffering.

In the heart of the village, Calista paused. The accumulated stories of anguish and resilience echoed in her mind. She realised that suffering was an inevitable companion on life's journey. However, it was not the antagonist but a mentor, sculpting hearts to embrace the symphony of emotions and fostering connections between souls.

Calista's moral was clear – in the tapestry of existence, suffering wove the threads of empathy, resilience, and compassion. It was a catalyst for personal growth and an invitation to extend a hand of understanding to fellow travellers. As Calista stood under the starlit sky, she whispered to the universe, "Suffering, though painful, is a master sculptor of the human spirit, chiselling away the superfluous to reveal the masterpiece within."

Adhrit probed deeper, "What are the causes of this suffering, Master?"

Shree Shambav, with unwavering patience, elaborated, "Resistance to impermanence, a sense of disconnection, clinging to a limited identity, a desire for a reality incongruent with the present, external validations, leading a divided life, external living, choosing fear over love, seeking certainty in an unpredictable world, dwelling in the past or future, playing the victim, prioritizing comfort over growth, neglecting self-care, and denying parts of oneself – these are the roots of suffering."

With each cause unveiled, the Shree Shambav urged Adhrit and the others to embark on an inner journey. "Recognise these sources," he emphasised, "and you can transmute suffering into a sacred odyssey of growth, acceptance, and self-love. Navigate discomfort, live authentically, choose love over fear, engage with the present, relinquish victimhood, and embrace growth over comfort. In doing so, you become the architect of your liberation."

Shree Shambav spoke with profound depth, "In the crucible of suffering, lessons of empathy, resilience, and the profound value of compassion emerge. It acts as an unyielding teacher, guiding us into the intricate realms of our emotions and fostering a profound comprehension of the journeys undertaken by those around us. Amidst the shadows of suffering, seeds of personal growth are sown, blossoming into increased strength and an unwavering appreciation for the brighter facets of life."

As the entourage continued their expedition through the landscapes of human tribulation, each story, like a page in an ancient manuscript, unfolded to reveal deeper layers of understanding. Shree Shambav's teachings resonated not merely as words but as profound echoes guiding them through the labyrinth of existence, where suffering, when acknowledged and harnessed, transformed into a stepping stone toward a life lived with purpose and enlightenment.

A Symphony of Soulful Suffering

In the crucible of knowing, where pain breaks free,

Shattered are the walls, revealing what's meant to be.

A symphony of suffering, echoing through the soul,

Each note is a piercing truth, making the broken whole.

Can you, in awe, embrace the bitter cup,

Where pain and joy entwine, and sorrows sup?

Accept the seasons, the heart's ebb and flow,

In grief's wintry silence, a resilient warmth may grow.

The self-chosen suffering, a bitter draught we sip,
The healer's potion, from life's sacred script.
Trust the unseen hands that guide our fate,
In the silent chamber, where the heart contemplates.

The cup, though aflame, holds tears divine,
A vessel moulded in the Potter's sacred design.
Within the crucible, where shadows dance and play,
Lessons of empathy and resilience find their way.

In the intricate tapestry of sorrow's embrace,
Seeds of growth are sown, finding solace and grace.
Amidst the shadows, where the heart takes flight,
Deeper emotions unfurl, on the canvas of the night.

Gems of understanding, forged in suffering's fire,
A profound journey, where the soul aspires.

In the silent echoes of pain's tender art,

A masterpiece born from the depths of the heart.

- Shree Shambav

Life Coach and Philanthropist

Shree Shambav is the visionary founder of the Shree Shambav Ayur Rakshita Foundation (www.shambav-ayurrakshita.org). He founded this institution with a lofty goal: to recognise human identity across gender, ethnicity, and nationality. Through this organisation, he wants to assist all communities in realising their full potential and the intrinsic beauty of life.

Shree Shambav, a Life Coach, is dedicated to supporting people on their journeys of self-discovery and empowerment. He assists people in discovering who they are, determining what inspires and drives them, and overcoming limiting ideas. His approach clarifies what one wants in life, assisting people through goal-setting and a step-by-step process for achieving them. He empowers people to make deliberate and responsible decisions, allowing them to identify their blind spots and evolve as individuals via the use of numerous strategies and tools.

The foundation's bold, uncompromising, and compassionate ventures are always aimed at initiating the "Inner Transformation" process. They focus on spiritual growth, personal growth, and self-healing while emphasising that true progress lies in "Inclusive Growth and Co-existence." This philosophy drives all their initiatives, encouraging a holistic approach to development and well-being.

Under Shree Shambav's leadership, the foundation has launched several impactful movements:

Shree Shambav Green Movement: This mission is to create a healthy, green, and clean earth through responsible water conservation and greening initiatives. The movement strives to make the world a green paradise by encouraging sustainable living and environmental responsibility.

Shree Shambav Vidya Vedhika (Vizhuthugal): This project aims to help students and children by offering training, books, stationery, and uniforms. It aims to provide the next generation with the tools and resources they need to excel both academically and personally.

Shree Shambav and his foundation exemplify the spirit of compassion, transformation, and inclusive growth via their work, which has a profound impact on individuals and communities around the world. His work exemplifies the power of acknowledging and nourishing the human spirit, creating a world in which everyone can reach their full potential and appreciate the beauty of life.

TESTIMONIALS

Journey of Soul - Karma - "We die in our twenties and are buried at eighty." Remember that nothing can stop someone who refuses to be stopped. "Most people do not fail; they simply give up." Shree Shambav deserves full credit. It allowed me to sit and consider what I might miss out on in life. The author has delved into every aspect of our daily lives. How can a seemingly insignificant change in these seemingly insignificant details bring us such joy? The Soul of Journey teaches you the "art of living" as well as the "art of dying."

Twenty + One Series - The rich cultural heritage offered a host in twenty + one short stories with incredible imagination, morals and values prevalent at a given time, influencing how people respond to a crisis or any situation. The author has recreated images with universal values and morals. The plentiful of fascinating from faraway lands would leave the modern play and story writers a cringe. The book supports trust and immeasurable values instilling hope for the new generations.

Death - "Shree Shambav's 'Death - Light of Life and the Shadow of Death' is an extraordinary masterpiece that delves deep into the profound questions surrounding our existence and mortality. The book's opening statement, 'Nothing ever truly dies; it simply ceases to exist in one form before resuming it in another,' sets the stage for a thought-provoking exploration of death's multifaceted nature. Shambav's remarkable ability to navigate the philosophical complexities of death and our universal fear of it is both enlightening and comforting. This book is a testament to the power of understanding and acceptance."

Whispers of Eternity - "Reading 'Whispers of Eternity' by Shree Shambav was a transformative experience that left me captivated from beginning to end. Each section of this exquisite collection delves into the myriad facets of existence, offering poignant reflections on life, death, and everything in between. Shree Shambav's verses are a testament to the beauty of language and the power of expression, inviting readers to embark on a journey of self-discovery and spiritual awakening. Whether celebrating life's simple joys or grappling with the complexities of human emotion, this book is a timeless companion that speaks to the heart and soul of every reader."

Life Changing Journey Series - "Life Changing Journey Series II Inspirational Quotes" is a remarkable collection that illuminates the path to self-discovery and personal growth. With its inspiring quotes and insightful reflections, this book serves as a beacon of light in a world often shrouded in darkness. Each quote offers wisdom, guidance, and encouragement, reminding readers of their inner strength and resilience. A must-read for anyone seeking inspiration and enlightenment.

Learn To Love Yourself – "A Heartfelt Guide to Authentic Self-Love." "Learn to Love Yourself" invites readers on a transformative journey to embrace their true essence in a world often focused on external validation. Through ten insightful chapters, it gently reveals principles of genuine self-love, guiding readers to deepen their connection with themselves. Beyond surface positivity, it encourages the cultivation of resilient self-acceptance, from embracing one's unique qualities to setting empowering boundaries. With inspiring stories and practical wisdom, this book is a trusted companion on the path to inner peace, fulfilment, and joy, helping readers build lives that reflect their authentic selves.

The Power of Letting Go – This book has been a gift to my spiritual journey. Shree Shambav's insights into attachment, personal growth cycles, and forgiveness are enlightening. The concept of seven-year cycles resonated with me, helping me understand the natural phases of life. I feel more empowered to let go of what no longer serves me and step into a life of freedom and fulfilment. A truly beautiful read!

A Journey of Lasting Peace – "A Journey of Lasting Peace" feels like a trusted friend guiding you through the maze of self-discovery. The 18 transformative principles are both practical and deeply resonant, addressing everything from gratitude practices to the art of letting go. Each chapter is infused with warmth and wisdom, making it easy to apply the concepts to my life. I particularly appreciated the emphasis on physical health's connection to mental well-being; it served as a wake-up call for me to prioritise my health. This book is an invaluable resource for anyone serious about personal growth!

Astrology Unveiled Series – "Profound, Logical, and Inspiring". What stands out in Astrology Unveiled is the author's dedication to making Vedic astrology logical and approachable. Each concept flows naturally into the next, backed by examples and exercises. The insights into karma and life cycles add a philosophical depth rarely seen in astrology books. Perfect for anyone seeking spiritual growth alongside astrological knowledge!

The Entitlement Trap - "Thought-Provoking and Challenging" The book challenges readers to confront their own sense of entitlement, and that's not easy—but it's essential. The Entitlement Trap doesn't offer a one-size-fits-all approach. Instead, it's a thoughtful, layered examination of how entitlement can limit our growth. The chapter on "Defining Your Own Hill" was particularly impactful, as it pushed me to reconsider which challenges are truly worth pursuing. A thought-provoking read for those willing to do the inner work to create a life they can be proud of.

Whispers of a Dying Soul – "A Soul-Stirring Reflection on Life's Unspoken Truths" **-** *Whispers of a Dying Soul: Unspoken Regrets and Unlived Dreams"* is a deeply moving exploration of the unexpressed emotions and unfulfilled aspirations that shape our lives in ways we often don't realise. This book invites readers to confront the powerful, often hidden impact of regret while guiding them through a journey of introspection and healing. Each page opens a space to reflect on the choices that define us—from moments of unspoken love to neglected passions—offering a gentle reminder to live authentically and courageously.

Whispers of the Soul: A Journey Through Haiku - is a mesmerising collection that speaks directly to the heart. Each haiku is a delicate brushstroke capturing life's fleeting beauty and timeless wisdom, inviting readers into moments of deep reflection and peace. This book is a balm for the soul, guiding us to find meaning in stillness and connection in simplicity. The themes of nature, love, and mindfulness echo universal truths, resonating with quiet, powerful grace.

It's a book to be savoured slowly, cherished deeply, and returned to often. Truly, a gift for anyone seeking calm and clarity in life's chaos.

Whispers of Silence - Unlocking Inner Power through Stillness by Shree Shambav is a rare gem that beckons readers to pause, reflect, and reconnect with their inner selves. In a world that never stops talking, this book offers a profound exploration of silence—not as a void but as a rich and transformative space.

From the first page, Shree Shambav's writing resonates deeply, blending scientific insights with spiritual wisdom in a way that feels both universal and deeply personal. The author's ability to bridge the tangible and the transcendent makes this book an invaluable guide for anyone navigating the chaos of modern life.

The Power of Words: Transforming Speech, Transforming Lives - "The Power of Words is a profound and enlightening guide that has transformed the way I approach communication. Shree Shambav masterfully uncovers the hidden influence of our words on relationships, self-perception, and overall well-being. This book doesn't just teach you how to speak; it inspires mindful communication that fosters connection and trust. The insights on replacing negative patterns like gossip and judgment with kindness and authenticity are truly life-changing. The practical strategies and engaging narratives make it an invaluable resource for personal and professional growth. A must-read for anyone striving to communicate with intention, clarity, and compassion. Highly recommended!"

The Art of Intentional Living: Minimalism for a Life of Purpose - "The Art of Intentional Living is a refreshing guide to finding clarity in a cluttered world. With practical wisdom and profound insights, it inspires you to simplify, prioritise, and live with purpose. A must-read for anyone seeking balance and fulfilment."

Awakening the Infinite: The Power of Consciousness in Transforming Life - "Awakening the Infinite is a transformative guide that expands the mind and nourishes the soul. With profound insights and practical wisdom, this book beautifully explores the power of consciousness, helping readers connect with their true purpose and inner potential. It is a journey of self-discovery, healing, and spiritual awakening, offering clarity and inspiration at every turn. A must-read for anyone looking to live with greater awareness, meaning, and authenticity."

Beyond the Veil: A Journey Through Life After Death:

"This book touched me in ways few others have—it's not just about death, but about life, meaning, and the vast unknown that connects them. Beyond the Veil offers a graceful blend of science and spirit, inviting us to explore the mystery with awe rather than fear. The stories, insights, and reflections linger in your heart long after the final page. A truly transformative read that brings light on the shadows of mortality. It reminded me that in embracing death, we truly learn how to live."

Bonds Beyond Blood:

"A profoundly moving story that reminds us family is not defined by blood, but by love, sacrifice, and the courage to heal. Every chapter touched my soul with its emotional truth and timeless wisdom. Through joy, grief, and redemption, this book captures the raw beauty of human connection. I saw reflections of my own family in its pages—both the pain and the hope. A powerful, unforgettable read that lingers long after the final word."

A Journey into Spiritual Maturity: 12 Golden Rules for Inner Transformation

"This book is a gentle yet powerful guide that awakened a deeper sense of purpose within me. Each golden rule felt like a mirror reflecting truths I needed to embrace. Shree Shambav's wisdom is timeless, poetic, and profoundly grounding. It's not just a read—it's a journey into the heart of who you truly are. A must-read for anyone seeking lasting peace, clarity, and inner transformation."

The Inner Battlefield: Overcoming the Enemies of the Mind and Soul:

"This book is a powerful revelation—an honest mirror to the battles we fight within. Every chapter is a step closer to clarity, peace, and emotional mastery. Shree Shambav brilliantly transforms ancient wisdom into practical guidance for modern souls. It awakened in me a new strength to face my fears and rise above inner turmoil. A must-read for anyone seeking true inner victory and lasting transformation."

The Seeker's Gold – Unlocking Life's Greatest Treasure

The Seeker's Gold is a soul-stirring masterpiece that goes far beyond the pursuit of wealth—it is a journey into the heart of what truly matters. Each chapter unfolds with poetic wisdom and emotional depth, revealing that life's real treasure is not found in riches but in the transformation of the self. As the protagonist evolves through trials, love, and profound realisations, so does the reader. This book is a mirror for every dreamer, a lantern for every seeker, and a companion for anyone walking the path of purpose. A timeless tale that stays with you long after the final page.

Born to Rise Series I & II:

Born to Rise – Series I & II is a profound awakening—a journey that begins in silence and leads you to the core of your true power.

Series I reshapes your understanding of success, showing that clarity is more valuable than applause, and authenticity more powerful than performance.

Series II takes you deeper, unlocking the mindset and inner strategy behind meaningful, lasting growth—not just in wealth, but in wisdom.

Together, these books are not just guides—they are soul mirrors, revealing the truths you've forgotten and the strength you've always held.

This is more than reading—it's remembering who you are, and rising with purpose, not pressure.

ACKNOWLEDGEMENTS

To my grandfathers, grandmothers, mothers, fathers, aunts, uncles, neighbours, sisters, brothers, friends, and teachers, they poured in endless moral stories, retellings of Ramayana, Mahabharata, Puranas, Upanishads, and so on.

My teachers, neighbours, and kindred souls. Who provided us with a stage to perform wonderful Puranic stories and were gracious enough to acknowledge our efforts.

The artists and translators of epics have served as a source of inspiration, invigorating our spirits, making these works accessible, and enabling us to grasp the profound depths and deeper dimensions they contain.

I also cherish the stimulating conversations; I had with my wonderful mothers, Punitha Muniswamy and Uma Devi.

Our family's youngest member, Aadhya, who always overwhelmed me with questions, inspired this book.

I would likewise prefer to express gratitude to Mr Sivakumar, Mrs Roopa Sivakumar, Mr Akshaya

Rajesh, Ms Akshatha Rajesh, Ms Apeksha Prabhu, Mr Akanksh Prabhu, Mr Nikash Sarasambi, Mrs Spoorthi Nikash for their valuable inputs.

I must thank Mr Rajesh, Mr Savan Prabhu, Mrs Revathi Rajesh, Mrs Rajani Sarasambi, and Mrs Manju Reshma, who encouraged me and often suggested writing a book. Their unwavering belief that I had something valuable to offer kept me going during my writing sessions.

Love you all,

Shree Shambav

www.shambav.org

shreeshambav@gmail.com

9 789334 351255

Printed at Repro India Ltd.